10 SMART MONEY MOVES FOR WOMEN

HOW TO CONQUER YOUR FINANCIAL FEARS

DR. JUDITH BRILES

CB
CONTEMPORARY BOOKS

Library of Congress Cataloging-in-Publication Data

Briles, Judith.
    10 smart money moves for women: how to conquer your financial
fears / Judith Briles.
      p. cm.
    ISBN 0-8092-2783-5
    1. Women—Finance, Personal. 2. Finance, Personal. I. Title.
HG179.B7278 1999
332.024'042—dc21
                                         99-17807
                                          CIP

Cover design by Scott Rattray
Cover art copyright © Digital Vision Ltd. All rights reserved. Image Club Graphics,
a division of Adobe Systems Inc.
Interior design by Precision Graphics

Published by Contemporary Books
A division of NTC/Contemporary Publishing Group, Inc.
4255 West Touhy Avenue, Lincolnwood (Chicago), Illinois 60712-1975 U. S. A.
Copyright © 1999 by The Briles Group, Inc.
Printed in the United States of America
International Standard Book Number: 0-8092-2783-5

00 01 02 03 04 LB 20 19 18 17 16 15 14 13 12 11 10 9 8 7 6 5 4 3 2

Woman to Woman 2000

The Confidence Factor

Gender Traps

The Briles Report on Women in Healthcare

Becoming a Woman of Confidence

Woman to Woman: From Sabotage to Support

When God Says No

Money $ense Guidebook

Money Sense

The Dollars and Sense of Divorce

The Workplace: Questions Women Ask

Raising Money-Wise Kids

The Dollars and Cents of Divorce

Financial Savvy for Women

Money Guide

Faith and $avvy, Too!

Money Phases

The Woman's Guide to Financial Savvy

For Dolores

Contents

Smart Money Move #7
Become the Expert   147

Foreword

The new millennium has created a wake-up call for anyone who earns, spends, saves, invests, or gives away money. The days of generous employer-paid pensions are bygone; the days of "no-worry" Social Security payouts are the twentieth century's dinosaurs; the days of being financially self-sufficient are the real world, no longer just a Hollywood movie.

For women, the pressure for financial independence is as great as it has ever been. That pressure increases with age and women's changing role in society. Outside of sales, there are few jobs that pay women at the same rate as men. Yet women do not have a lesser need for money than men. The mere fact that you are holding this book aligns you with the majority of what women report—85 percent wished they had learned more about money and investing while growing up.

Dr. Judith Briles's *10 Smart Money Moves for Women* will guide you through the many money-related fears that women of all ages have expressed. Some of these fears stem from their upbringing, others through misadventures in working and investing money. These are fears that include being broke to even being too successful. These fears are not specific to just women and can be overcome with the awareness that they exist and why. If you are willing to learn some of the new tools and techniques that are presented in this friendly, hands-on book, then you are on your way to eliminating your financial fears.

10 Smart Money Moves for Women will teach you practical, simple tips that will guide you away from some of the most common mistakes people

make with their money today. This book will show you how to create and
maintain a realistic financial plan, what insurance pitfalls to avoid, how to
build a tithe to yourself, how to invest for fun and for profit, which advisors to use and not to use, how to use other people's money wisely, how to
recover when you make mistakes, and how to become your own expert.

At Hantz Financial Services, our goal is to help people achieve their
financial goals by offering choices from a variety of services and products
to meet every investment need. *10 Smart Money Moves for Women* parallels
our goals. By following the various strategies within these pages, you will
find that you will not only reach your own goals but that you will do it as
a savvy traveler along today's financial expressway—one who now understands that many of the roadblocks contained in the money maze can be
jumped over, around, and sometimes through. Owning this book is your
first Smart Money Move.

John R. Hantz
CEO and President
Hantz Financial Services

Judith's Story

People who write books on money come from two backgrounds—writing financial newsletters, columns, and books, or advising individuals as financial professionals, as their stockbrokers, certified financial planners, registered investment advisors, and so forth.

I come from both sides. Today I'm a writer, speaker, and consultant. Prior to donning those hats, I worked exclusively in the field of money advice. Most of my clients were women—some with lots of money, some with very little. In 1986 I decided to dedicate myself to speaking and writing about money and a few other topics that I had returned to school to research.

What brought me to the money field was a divorce. I had watched my "heart mom" go through one. Joyce was the stereotype of an affluent homemaker: four kids, beautiful home, pool, horses, country club membership, and weekly bridge games with the "girls"—other women who enjoyed similar lifestyles. Her experience with money at that time was limited to spending it—by either writing checks or pulling out her credit card.

All her bills were paid on time—she told her husband what the grand tally was at the end of the month, and he put the necessary funds in her bank account. That all changed when she went through a divorce after twenty-five-plus years of marriage. It was horrifying to watch her stumble in some areas and to see family members take advantage of her softness, generosity, and naiveté. I learned later that her oldest son, the person I referred to in later years as "my children's father" or "training husband," had manipulated thousands of dollars from her. I vowed that it would never happen to me or my daughters.

Two years after Joyce's divorce, I followed down her footsteps. I was in her shoes and felt lucky to have my sanity and physical health when I left a ten-year marriage. *The only difference was that she had money and I had none when the divorce was over.* My ex-husband created a nightmare for me and just about anyone that I interacted with. He harassed my friends and my employer. I ended up getting fired from a job that I liked, did well at, and made good money from. The manager of the office gave me a two-week severance after my ex had called the office several times and threatened him and my immediate boss. The manager said to me, "Have you considered moving? He will make your life hell until you get some distance between you."

That was in the 1970s. (If I had known then what I know today, I would never have been fired—but that was then; this is now.) I headed to northern California, putting more than 400 miles between us. The brokerage firm of E.F. Hutton hired me in the early 1970s as a stockbroker. Having at least one woman in the office seemed the politically correct thing to do at that time. Initially, all my clients were men. Within a few years that changed as word spread that there was a woman broker who would "talk and explain" investments to women. I began to teach classes on women and money in the community. Both E.F. Hutton and I did well during our five-year relationship.

Within a few years, my net worth exceeded a million dollars—a big leap for someone who had no money just a few years before. I remarried, and life looked pretty good . . . until I discovered that a friend and partner had embezzled several hundred thousand dollars from a loan for which I was personally liable. I had signed a bank note that guaranteed the funds. By the time everything was over, my (and my family's) financial life was a disaster—probably material for a movie of the week!

We were broke. Our beautiful home was gone, and we had to sell our cars, liquidate all our investments at fire-sale prices, and even sell clothes to keep food on the table for three hungry teenagers. Top Ramen noodles were a daily staple—cheap and filling. In the middle of the mess, I had three surgeries (one for cancer) and my nineteen-year-old son died in an accident. Life was not a joy. There were many times when I just didn't want to go on. I was really at the bottom—broke mentally, physically, and financially. This was not a good place for the primary breadwinner to be.

By applying the principles in this book, the ones that I have taught to so many, we survived and recovered. Will we have over a million dollars again? I don't know. But I do know that by dealing with our fears and using smart money tools, we came through without relying on any type of government assistance or handouts. Five years after I hit the financial rock bottom, my husband and I were able to buy a home and start rebuilding our retirement funds.

My memories of the many clients and their fears never left me. Throughout *10 Smart Money Moves for Women*, I use examples from my own life as well as from the lives of thousands of clients that I have worked with—you may even find yourself looking in the mirror.

Judith Briles
Summer 1999

Acknowledgments

Books never get written by themselves—they are always a team effort. My team consisted of agent Jeff Herman, who embraced the idea over a phone call. Editors Susan Schwartz and Danielle Egan-Miller were supportive throughout, pushing me when I needed to be pushed. Susan Moore-Kruse followed up on all my questions, no matter how small.

Staff members Karen Zuppa, Shori Wilson, and Dolores Hall eagerly gave their input when asked (and sometimes when not). As always, husband John Maling encouraged me to just get it done, noting along the way as he read each completed chapter that this new child, *10 Smart Money Moves for Women,* delivers what is needed in a commonsense approach to working with money.

I thank them all.

Smart Women and Money

This book is about money. It's also about women—specifically, their gaining the confidence to use, handle, and invest money. To many, these are glaring contradictions of terms, and that's why this book is necessary. Even today women have not fully earned strong respect or recognition as money managers.

Oppenheimer Funds conducted a nationwide survey that looked at the investing habits of men and women. The 1997 survey showed the following:

- In couples living/planning together, most women are responsible for the day-to-day management of household finances. Sixty-two percent balance the checkbook, 58 percent pay all the bills, and 44 percent maintain a household budget.

- Only 15 percent of the women surveyed made investment decisions on their own, as compared with 38 percent of the men.

- More than 60 percent of the women surveyed said they didn't understand how a mutual fund works.

- Fewer than 13 percent of women describe themselves as "very knowledgeable" when it comes to investing.

- Of the 1,000-plus women interviewed, 85 percent "wished they had learned more about money and investing growing up."

- Of the women who stated that they didn't invest, the primary reasons cited were "they had no money to invest" or "they didn't know where to begin."
- When men and women were asked who was the more knowledgeable, only 13 percent of the women and 6 percent of the men said that women are. Almost half of all the men and women surveyed said that men are more knowledgeable, and approximately 30 percent said that men and women are equally knowledgeable about investments.

It is interesting to note that women and men report that they set investment goals and interact with financial advisors on a similar basis. When it comes to selecting savings and investment options and managing their savings and investments, however, men continue to take charge in these areas. One of the eye-openers in the survey relates to respect. Only 25 percent of the respondents believed that stockbrokers and financial planners treated women with the same level of respect that men received. This is not good news for women.

To set goals and interact with advisors is definitely a good start, but there is so much more. You can't stop at goal setting; you must implement a strategy that matches the goals that have been defined. When women choose not to be involved in selecting investments and then monitoring and managing them, they become incredibly vulnerable to outside pressures that may not be in their own best financial interest.

Look around you. Who are your friends, neighbors, coworkers, relatives, even parents of your children's friends? Do they have perfect lives? Is everything running smoothly in their households—no problems at home or work, tragedies, separations, or divorces? Is this the real world? I don't think so. Problems and bad news are everywhere—maybe not right under your roof, but with someone you know. And believe it or not, money becomes a factor.

It's ironic that women have proved that they can do almost anything. Women work in numerous male-dominated occupations, as doctors, dentists, lawyers, engineers, pilots, police, and CEOs. In fact, almost 50 percent of medical, dental, and legal school students are female today. Many have become "superwomen," balancing work and family in the most remarkable ways. Today's woman has stretched and become knowledgeable in a variety of areas. Yet in one of the single most important areas of American society—financial independence and confidence—too many remain woefully uninformed and uncertain.

Yes, many of us talk to advisors and make plans and goals. But it is not enough. Whether you are a single woman or have a partner, you must learn the various components of investing: which investments are suitable for specific goals and which are not. The learning curve comes from the selection and management of one's investments, not from abdicating those tasks to someone else.

If you are single, you may not marry. If you are married, you may become widowed or divorced. Today, the latest statistics from insurance companies reveal that on the average women outlive men by seven years. That means that probably at some time in your adult life you will be on your own. Decisions that relate to money management will rest in your hands. Are you prepared for that day, a day that could become many years?

To be ignorant of money workings is to remain a powerless outsider to an enormously significant aspect of daily life. By failing to participate in long-term money management, a woman can end up abdicating her power and right to be financially aware and independent. Most people, especially women, wait for a life-altering event as their wake-up call. Why wait for a crisis to propel you into taking charge of your finances?

> Financial confidence and independence are critical for all women.

WHY NOT WOMEN AND MONEY?

It is not uncommon for a woman to be an expert in science, engineering, or marketing and still not know what to do with her earnings, her savings, her investments. In an interview with a major newspaper in Michigan in the late fall of 1998, a reporter shared that she had done a survey of all the women in her newsroom. She announced that the women fit the profile of the Oppenheimer survey—they handled the day-to-day money management, yet didn't have a lot to do with investments. They relied on others—spouse, parents, relatives, even friends—instead of learning for themselves about investment programs and strategies.

We women are very trusting; we forget that other people make mistakes too. Worse, they sometimes die or become disabled or are lost through divorces. They may not always be there for us.

Some women are satisfied with the ease of savings accounts or with letting a professional—the friendly banker or insurance agent—be their guide. But, don't forget—that bankers have vested interests of their own, that inflation often runs higher than bank interest rates, or that bankers, too, make mistakes.

Women must be involved with money for the simple reason that they are around it more often than men are. How, you might think? Here's how, according to the General Accounting Office of the U.S. Government in 1997:

- Women outlive men by at least seven years. The average age of first-time widowhood is fifty-five.

- The present divorce rate for first-time marriages is 47 percent and is 49 percent for second marriages.

- Women often earn less than men do and change jobs more frequently, usually in the pursuit of making more money.

- Seventy-five percent of the elderly persons living below the poverty level are women. A great many of them have Social Security as their *sole* source of funds.

- Women are much more likely than men to leave their jobs to care for family members—their own children and their parents.

- Eighty percent of the widows presently living in poverty were not poor prior to their husband's death.

How important is the Social Security issue? Quite. According to the Social Security Administration and the National Commission on Retirement Policy, 44 million Americans depended on it in 1998. For two-thirds of them, it was their *main* source of income. For one out of five, it was their *only* income. If there was no Social Security, half of all retirees would live below the poverty level. Does this impact women? You bet! It's a key, if not the main, source of retirement income—1998's average check was $745!

When Social Security was started in the thirties, there were far fewer retirees withdrawing funds than now and far more paying in. The money just flowed in. That has changed. Most likely, payments will be trimmed back when the huge number of baby boomers begin to retire. For women, and men, it means that every one of us must commit to making our money grow, starting today.

> A recurring fear for many women is that they will be broke when they stop working or, if married, when their spouses die.

On the threshold of a new millennium, it seems surprising that some women still view money management as unfeminine. A woman who actively pursues money management is deemed aggressive and pushy. Many parents and teachers discourage girls from taking an interest in money and numbers. They also discourage them from a more elementary financial necessity—the willingness to take risks. The penalties for mischief or adventurous misbehavior tend to be far greater for girls than for boys, who are still expected and encouraged to be more aggressive and daring.

Another deterrent has been that women are traditionally "right-brain" thinkers. Professionals who study the brain tell us that its right side tends to control passion, intuition, dreams, and feelings. A woman is more apt to act from instinct than from the strictly rational, logical, "left-brain" mode that is more dominant in men. The right-brain thinker is more creative, often a generalist, and usually less predictable and more personable than the left-brain thinker.

Since the financial world has been dominated by the more dependable, objective, deductive, left-brain reasoning of males, women have not been taken as seriously as men have been. Only recently have greater numbers of women bought homes in their name alone. Even though many thousands of women own successful companies, many banks still consider women "unfit" for large-scale dealings. It's goofy thinking, but still out there.

Society can undermine your rights and abilities to participate in long-term financial management. You really don't need a Ph.D. to understand why some women lack confidence about finance management and shy away from strategy making. Yet it is imperative that couples communicate openly about money—their concerns, fears, hopes, and dreams.

The good news is that society, at last, is changing, and the money mystique is breaking down. The short-term skills of family finances are not so different from the long-term skills of financial planning. At times women may actually have an advantage over men in the money game. After all, we have shopped for years, and the same skills that help us choose the best goods in a market can be applied to the stock exchange. The majority of household budgets are run by women. The bottom line is that women do *think* about money—what they are currently doing or not doing with it and what they would do if they had more of it.

> It is time women added their unique genius to the money game.

Women have shown they can make money; now they must recognize the importance of managing it as well. For too long women have worked for their money, letting it manage them. The woman of the twenty-first century must now make her money work for her. That's you. You will learn how to get money working for you by using the *10 Smart Money Moves* in this book.

SMART MONEY MOVES MONEY PROFILE

Before reading the first chapter, rate yourself with the Smart Money Moves Money Profile to see where you currently are in your money emotions. Mark (1) for *always,* (2) for *often,* (3) for *sometimes,* and (4) for *never.*

1. I like to talk about money.

2. I regularly save money.

3. I am interested in different ways to invest.

4. I am optimistic about my finances.

5. I know what my annual income is.

6. I know how much I made during the previous year.

7. I know the amount I pay in taxes.

8. I know what it costs me to live monthly.

9. I feel that I can take care of myself financially.

10. I know how much I contribute to retirement each year.

11. I know how much is in my checking account.

12. I spend money to make myself feel better.

13. I max my credit cards to their limits.

14. If I died tomorrow, my affairs would be in order.

15. If I get a tax refund, it is never more than $100.

SCORING:

46–60 You are in the *Red Zone of Money*. Depending on your age (the younger you are), you may feel that you have few money issues or concerns. After all, you have a lifetime ahead of you. The reality is that as youth creeps by, money, especially the lack of it, suddenly becomes a critical factor in your life. You have major work ahead to avert the high risk of disaster that may loom down your path.

28–45 You are in the *Yellow Zone of Money*—put on the brakes and take a close look at what you are doing. You are not in a disaster zone yet, but your so-so attitude and lack of attention could permanently set you up for fiscal failure.

15–27 You've got the go signal and are in the *Green Zone of Money*. You are fairly savvy when it comes to your money habits. The lower your score, the more bravos head your way. Don't let your good habits slide.

Face Your Money Fears

1

You aren't born with a fear of or an attitude about money, but it's guaranteed that you've got a few. Fears and attitudes—be they good, bad, or ugly—have been developed over a period of time. No doubt, your upbringing is a major contributing factor. Past experiences—successes and failures—create the flooring. Then there's society—always ready to jump in and give its two bits worth via the media, your circle of friends, practices that are widely accepted or tolerated, your family, or even the government.

Let's face it. You are the steward of your money—however big or small your pocketbook or stash, you are in charge of its destiny . . . at least its initial leg of the money journey.

> You will decide whether you consume money, grow it, or give it away.

USING MONEY

Does money buy happiness? Many people think so, especially the young and those who have received lump sums that usually come as gifts. That belief doesn't last long. Money can be a trap. It's easy to say "If I only had more income (savings, investments, real estate, etc.), I would be happier (more comfortable, satisfied, joyful, generous, etc.)." Really? Let's find out.

Read the columns below. Circle or underline all the words that most sound like where you are or how you feel today.

1	2	3	4	5
Unhappy	Unproductive	Steady	Happy	Joyful
Insecure	Barely coping	Average	Tension-free	Accomplished
Angry	Not good enough	Ordinary	Aspiring	Acknowledged
Lonely		OK	Secure	Valued
Need love	Not having enough	Accepted	Fun	Powerful
Inhibited		Satisfied	Pleased	Confident
Unfinished	Improving	Common	Peaceful	Exhilarated
Uncomfortable	Searching	Worthy	Competent	Blissful
Disappointed	Making do	Likable	Prepared	Excited
Fatigued	Struggling	Agreeable	Capable	Passionate
Low self-esteem	Needing assurance	Relationships OK	Productive	Making a difference
	Tense			
	Relationships need improving			

Now, how much income do you have per month—$0 to $1,000; $1,001 to $2,000; $2,001 to $3,000; $3,001 to $4,000; or over $4,000? If you compared your income and column number with a hundred, even a thousand other people, the result would surprise you. In real life most people, no matter how much they make or how much money they have, will be to the left of the "Average" in column #3! In other words, having a lot of money does not guarantee happiness.

Granted, it's good to know that there may not be concerns about food and shelter, but happiness—feeling content and valued as a person—comes in other denominations.

THE FEAR OF BEING POOR

In 1985 one of *USA Today*'s headlines read "Bag Lady Fears Drive Women to Stash Cash." Not a lot has changed for many women since I clipped that gem for my "nudge" file. The number one fear that women shared during the past year in my workshops is that they will be broke when they are older.

Years ago a client asked me if I would take the time to go see his mother. He told me that she had some investments and lived mostly off her dividends, interest, and monthly social security. He asked that I just check to see if she was getting a decent return on her portfolio. Nothing seemed unusual from his synopsis of her situation.

I made the appointment and spent a pleasant two hours getting to know Martha. She was in her early sixties at the time, was healthy, and believed that she was a good steward for her money. With financial data filled out, I promised to get back to her within the week with an update on several stocks and suggestions for any changes. As I got up to leave, Martha said, "What about my stash?"

"Stash," I responded, "what stash?"

She proceeded to point to the corner of her living room. All I saw was a big green, overstuffed chair. "My stash . . . in the chair . . . and drapes." This was a first for me—a whole new stash, rainy day, liquidity fund (more on that later) vehicle! My new client had stashed in excess of $30,000 over the years in her overstuffed green chair with matching draperies. She had lived through the Depression—never again would she or her family be without food if bad times hit again. It took me more than a year to convince her to move her money to a money market fund that would earn her interest.

Did she move the entire amount? Nope, at least not initially. Her bottom line was that she insisted on a stash of $5,000 in the house, money that she could tap into for a movie, food, play, repairs, anything. The good news is that she did move the rest to interest-bearing accounts. She signed up for check-writing privileges, and after two years she finally accepted the fact that she really could access her money by writing a check and depositing it into her regular checking account.

> Only 2 out of every 100 seniors sixty-five
> or older are financially independent.

Is being poor really a concern for today's woman? You bet. Government statistics show that for every 100 women and men who reach age sixty-five, only two are financially independent. How do the remainder make it? By relying on relatives, the government, or friends, or by working until they die. What a bleak prospect in what today seems a society of overall prosperity.

Women live longer than men do—which means in simple words that women are more likely to spend far more years just barely getting by than men are if they don't get involved in the money maze. Forget about the

White Knight rescuing you. It's a myth created by the media, primarily TV. Remember *Leave It to Beaver, Father Knows Best, The Brady Bunch,* even the cartoon series *The Flintstones?* No matter what the problem, the male in the household bailed everyone out. Whether the problem was emotional or financial, the dude at the top always had the solution.

The reality is that whether you are rich, poor, or in between, the person that you are going to have to rely on the most to keep *you* from the poorhouse is yourself—your creativity, your imagination, your intuition, and your smarts.

THE FEAR OF LOSING MONEY

At some point, everyone loses money. It can be from a bad investment, misplaced moneys, the erosion of inflation, failure to act or make a decision, fear of making the wrong decision, or fear of losing a job or other resource of funds. I know: I've done them all. When I was seven years old, I lived at the beach. I went to the corner Green Store (the building was painted green!) to get Popsicles for my four friends on a weekend afternoon. They had given me enough money to get one for each of us.

On my way home, I was intrigued by a guy who was making chalk pictures on the sidewalk and decided to watch him perform his magic. Before I knew it, the Popsicles were dripping through the bag. Our treats had melted, and so had the money I had been entrusted with. I thought about telling them that the bully down the street had stolen the goodies from me as I left the store, but decided against it.

Instead, I hit the beach and approached everyone who was drinking a soda. Could I have their empty bottles (this was before the days of cans, when returning pop bottles was rewarded with a deposit refund)? Before I knew it I had collected enough bottles at two cents each to trade in at the corner grocery store for new Popsicles. I learned that day that lost money can often be replaced through a little work.

Losing money is scary. Women are more fearful of losing money than men are.

Men usually make more money than women do in the workplace so if money is lost in a bad investment, a common male attitude is that it can be replaced. Earning less money, women are less likely to take the financial positions and risks that men often do. A lot of it has to do with familiarity—

from childhood, males get the predominant share of money messages from their families, friends, and peers.

I can remember my brothers buying old wrecks, fixing them up, and reselling them—*for a profit.* I didn't know that they were investing; for that matter, they probably didn't think of it that way either, yet that's what they were doing. My money experience was buying something, and, if I was lucky, it was on sale. The word *reselling* wasn't in my vocabulary.

Working with and investing money does not have to start in giant steps. In fact, it's wise to avoid them. Start with small steps. Whether it's putting money in a mutual fund (many funds allow you to start with as little as $100, if you commit to putting in a minimal amount on a monthly basis), a money fund, or a fund for the kids (or yourself), small amounts can build into fortunes.

Starting small allows you to learn along the way. A little here, a little there. If some of the "little" doesn't work out—the investment fails or never grows in value (also a failure)—you and your net worth won't be destroyed, which is much preferred to waking up one morning to a phone call that informs you that the one investment you made is gone and that your perceived net worth has plummeted or disappeared.

THE FEAR OF LOOKING STUPID

No one wants to appear or feel foolish. Yet, when it comes to money strategies and decisions, many women fear that the wrong move or outcome will announce to friends, family, and relatives that they blew it and really don't know what they are doing. Women envision trumpets heralding their mistakes or disaster. Of course, that doesn't happen; it just feels like it.

> Feeling stupid is often accompanied by a loss or a missed opportunity.

Financial fears are very real. And probably you don't like to talk about them. It's easier to shove them under the rug or out the door, hoping that they will all go away. But they rarely do.

The good news about money mistakes is that they can be incredible learning opportunities once the crisis has passed. You aren't stupid because the mistake happened. Once you become more confident with yourself in your decisions (and accept that you will stumble once in awhile), you will be able to assess your financial situation fairly quickly and begin to find remedies and cures. It doesn't happen overnight.

THE FEAR OF TALKING ABOUT MONEY

Your upbringing will most likely be the primary factor that shapes your money practices. Remember the Oppenheimer survey—85 percent of the women surveyed "wished" that they had had training and guidance about money and investing during their upbringing. *Most* women grew up in homes that avoided discussions about money. Or there was talk about money, but rarely discussions of it. Women report that "they felt out of the loop" when it came to *really* talking about money.

It is not uncommon for today's woman to carry on that practice within her family and in her own life. Sometimes the attitude becomes "If I don't talk about it or acknowledge it, it won't be a problem in my life."

If you come from one of those families that actively included discussions about money and its many facets, good for you. But realize that you are in the minority. Not all of your friends will be on the same wavelength as you are in money matters. Your awareness, and possibly your confidence about the topic, may actually intimidate them!

> Do you have a friend who is money savvy? If you do, ask her (or him) if she will mentor you in learning the most effective ways to manage money. Don't forget to ask her what kind of mistakes she has made and what she learned from them.

Over the years, I have conducted national studies on a variety of topics. One such topic has been confidence—what is it, where does it come from, and what is needed to increase it? In a nutshell, confidence is defined (after 4,000 women shared their thoughts) as *the power to create the regard, appreciation, and caring that you have for you.*

Where does confidence come from? "The baptism of fire" might summarize the thousands of women—making mistakes, a few failures along the way, and learning. How does this all apply to you and your overcoming any fears you might have of talking about money? Same thing—you will stumble here and there. By talking about it, by sharing your experiences and outcomes with other women and men, you will find that the money boat is quite large. Most of your women friends probably came from families where money chats weren't on the daily menu. You've got a lot of company!

THE FEAR OF MAKING MISTAKES AND FAILING

Every woman makes mistakes. I wish I had $10 for each one I've made over the past fifty-plus years. Although most women have had what they consider more than their fair share in the mistake and failure departments, that doesn't erase the stigma they fear mistakes and failures can bring. Few enjoy talking about their failures, yet there are lots of smart people who fail big time.

> Mistakes happen. You get to choose—will they cripple and paralyze you? Or will you look at them as occasions for learning and growth and experience?

There's no question that if you do make a mistake with your money, you aren't going to be happy about it. You may be ticked at the person who recommended you do what you did that didn't work out (including yourself). You may even create an internal dialogue with yourself—saying, telling, promising yourself that "if" a situation like this ever comes again, you won't do it or get caught again. As you approach the final stages, you accept what has happened—it doesn't mean you like it or approve of it. It means that you can't change what has happened and that you are ready to move on. Letting go means exactly that. It's over. You can't rewind the clock and get your money back. Letting go enables you to move on.

What you have to guard against is the reaction that the fear of failure and making mistakes can generate—paralysis. Getting stuck mentally. Making money mistakes and experiencing failures won't destroy you. Your key to resurrecting yourself is determining

- what happened;
- what factors you can control, influence, or alter;
- what factors you cannot control; and
- what you learned about the pros and cons of the money strategy.

THE FEAR OF CREATING
AND STICKING TO A PLAN

How many incredibly lucky people do you know that win money—lots of it? I bet very few, if any. None of my friends, acquaintances, colleagues, or the 20,000-plus women I speak to each year has ever told me that she has won big money. In fact, no one has ever told me that she has won more than a few hundred dollars playing blackjack or the slots in Las Vegas.

So, unless you are going to write and tell me that you are the exception—that you have hit it BIG, I'm going to assume that you have to make your money the old-fashioned way—earn it and invest it. It all starts with creating a plan and sticking to it.

> Creating a plan means making a commitment *to yourself*. And that's where the fear factor enters. If your plan is in writing, it means that you are supposed to do it rather than just talk about doing it. And, granted, that can be scary.

My speaking colleagues who work with groups on goal setting and time management tell me that one of the best ways to get started on anything is to put it in writing. Once "it" is in writing, it is easier to track, measure, and evaluate the author's progress—yours. Financial plans are guide tools that start you on a path that, if followed, will lead you to your stated money goals. They are not, though, set in granite. Times and circumstances change. So do investments and investment opportunities. That means that you don't create your plan and stick it in the drawer. It means you review it at least once a year.

You can create a financial plan in one of two ways—do it yourself or hire a professional. I opt for the professional, preferably for a certified financial planner. If you do it yourself, the only thing that will get in the way is you; if you hire a planner, a road map will be designed for you. The next step is that it's up to you to put your foot on the gas and get going—the commitment part.

THE FEAR OF BORROWING MONEY

Ideally, you would like to pay cash for everything. What's ideal and what's practical, however, are not always on the same track. Sometimes it makes sense to borrow money. Unless you have a big savings account, borrowing money to buy a home is a necessity. Having too much of a good thing can be bad. Overborrowing and too much credit are quite common. Borrowing too much should be feared. It's easy to get out of control.

Weekly, your mailbox probably has offerings of new credit cards—the deal of the week! Should you sign on? It depends. Ask yourself these questions:

- Do you need the credit? (It makes sense to have at least one credit card.)
- If you carry a balance, is the interest rate lower than the one(s) you presently have?
- If you don't carry a balance, what's the incentive for you to switch?

Most women who fear using credit carry that fear or belief over from their upbringing or from being married to someone who was out of control in using credit. If your family believed that everything was to be paid for by *cash* and that you didn't get it until you could pay for it, that could spook you about using any type of credit. If you were married to someone who created piles of debt everywhere he (and you) turned, then it would be natural to react negatively against any type of debt.

Both situations are extreme. Homes cost a lot of money; coming up with a down payment is not an easy task for many people. Cars aren't cheap, nor are retraining and education. Most women and men tap into credit resources for assistance.

The reality is that there is a balance in and to borrowing.

If you have borrowed or are contemplating borrowing money for a large item—a home or an educational loan—increase each payback amount by 10 percent. You will reduce the time it takes to pay back your loan by approximately one-third. That means you save big dollars and limit the time you "owe" someone. In the case of credit cards, use them by only charging the amount you will pay back within the grace period in which you get your bill. That way, no interest will be charged.

There is no question that the average overall debt burden is growing and that it can mentally and fiscally collapse a person. Here's some good news about women: according to the American Bankers Association, they are more likely to pay back borrowed money than men are.

In determining whether you should borrow or not, ask yourself if you need the item or only want it. If you *want* it, and could pay off the debt if you borrowed the cost over the designated time, don't purchase it. If you *need* the item, and can pay it off over the determined payoff time, purchase it. In reality, most people get in trouble when they let their wants dictate how credit is used.

THE FEAR OF INVESTING

Anyone who was awake as the new millennium approached knows that the stock market (at the time of this writing) was hot—it seemed as though everyone and anybody was making money. So, which way should you go—stocks, bonds, mutual funds, real estate, business opportunities? The list of possibilities is long.

One of the scary things about investing is that there are no guarantees. Any money that you invest can increase in value, maintain its original value, or decline in value. For women, the latter makes sleeping at night difficult. Because women have traditionally been paid less in the work-force, if their investments don't pan out, they are tremendously fearful that the moneys lost will never be replaced. It will take them longer to make up for the loss than it would for men.

Women are correct. It doesn't matter if they are paid $20,000 a year ($10 an hour) or $500,000 a year ($250 an hour); women make less than most men do at the same job, even when they have the same education, tenure, skills, and productivity. Catalyst, a New York–based firm that tracks working women, specifically executive working women, released a finding in the fall of 1998 about senior executive women who were making $500,000 while their male counterparts made more than $700,000 for the same job—these incredibly competent women were making only sixty-eight cents for each dollar their male colleagues made.

> Letting go of cash and possibly freezing money for an indefinite period of time to make more (or possibly lose) money create high levels of anxiety for many women.

So, do you throw in the towel and give up? Absolutely not. Over time, which means you start investing now, some investments outperform other investments. The stock market (versus investing in gemstones) is a classic example. One of the Momisms of life is "Be patient, your turn will come." Investing takes time and patience. When it comes to investing, don't focus on what your investment is worth this week, this month, this year. Concentrate on the long haul—what are the projections for five, ten years from now?

THE FEAR OF TRUSTING YOURSELF AND KEEPING THE WRONG ADVISORS

For women, it is not uncommon to be more loyal to money advisors—bankers, lawyers, accountants, realtors, insurance agents, stockbrokers, and financial planners—than to their own money. For women, it is also common to defer action and recommendations of what to do with their money to others. There are two key differences between men and women when it comes to money advisors.

- Women tend to form a type of friendship with their advisors, not wanting to terminate the relationship even if there are signs of poor advice or management.
- Some women too willingly abdicate financial decisions to someone else. They rarely follow up on what is suggested or done to their accounts. This is a direct result of upbringing influences.

In the fifteen years I advised women and men about their money, my goal was to get them involved, to have them not advocate their investment and money strategy decisions to me or to any other advisor. I understood their fears of making mistakes and looking stupid—after all, I had made my share of them and was fairly confident that I would probably make a few more on the journey down life's path. Most women run the day-to-day financial lives of their households. The world of investments, insurance, and the use of credit are not incredibly complicated. It takes time to work through the maze of options. Advisors can help—and so can *you*. Think of all the times you have said, "I *knew* it was the right thing to do," or "I *knew* it was going to happen." Trust yourself.

THE FEAR OF BEING TOO SUCCESSFUL

Many women are actually fearful of being too successful. They may be in a relationship and believe that "the man is supposed to make the decisions."

It doesn't matter if the man is the spouse, father, rich uncle, or the banker—just so it's a man. When women fear that their relationship will be jeopardized by their financial successes, what they're really talking about is power and control.

Traditionally, men have held the power and control of money management, investment, and decisions related to money and business. Today, a woman will be single for more years than she will be in a coupled relationship. Women are postponing marriage, if they marry at all, and they are the ones most likely to become widowed. If they do marry but then divorce, they will most likely remain in the single/divorced mode for several years before marrying again, if they do.

> Therapists who counsel couples report that even when the woman is the dominant breadwinner, she is less comfortable than her husband with leading the way in the financial arena.

Male and female styles of decision making may be at the crux here. Men are more inclined to make decisions on their own. It doesn't matter if it's a large or small purchase. Women take the opposite mode—they prefer to consult with their partner and may feel hurt or angry if a decision is made without their input. Men don't understand what the big deal is. These differences are so ingrained that changing them is difficult. For couples, the better route is to understand that there are differences, to be sensitive to them, and to create a type of relationship in which money talks can be constructive, not destructive.

Within couples, personality and style differences overflow to money management, investments, and decisions. On my radio show, *Smart Money Moves,* it is quite common to get several calls a month from listeners who say their husbands handle most of the family investment decisions. In probing, I learn that the results can range from mediocre to horrible. When the caller is asked why her spouse continues to make investments when his track record is bad, the reply is either "It's always been that way," "His feelings [my translation—ego] will get hurt," "I have good ideas about different investments, but if he doesn't believe they are his, he shoots them down," or "I don't want to take over and do better than he has—he will feel [that ego again] bad."

Please, please, please! Stop this nonsense. Everyone has talents—artistic, using gadgetry, intellectual, behavioral—dozens, hundreds of talents. Some might even involve money—its management and investment. Talents may be genetic or learned, but rarely do they come from being a specific gender.

If you are good at working with money—good at identifying investment possibilities and strategies—go to the head of the class. People rarely die from being too successful. In the money arena being successful means that your family, the people you care for and love, and you will be able to financially take care of yourselves. You *want* to be successful.

WHAT ARE YOUR FEARS?

Every woman has at least one money fear. For that matter, so do men. It's time to confront your deepest financial fears and get them out in the open. Becoming a bag lady is at the top of many lists. So is the fear that you will have to rely on others to put food on the table and shelter over your head. The fear of making a mistake that is financially catastrophic can paralyze you. Start identifying your fears. Write them down. Just the mere fact that they are on paper opens the door for you to confront them head-on.

As a motivational speaker, I am most frequently asked to talk about confidence—how to get it, recover it, and make it grow. There are many steps to building confidence; three of them are to learn something new, create positive thinking, and assess the situation.

As you proceed through the money maze with this book, you will learn new things—about yourself and others and how you and they relate to money. Learning new things enables you to look into your backpack of fears and do some assessing:

- Are my fears realistic in today's environment?
- Are they relevant to what I currently do?
- Do they hinder me from moving on?
- Are they life threatening (to my partner, my kids, my job, my friends, me)?

By identifying your fears, you are doing something quite positive. It's a big plus for you to acknowledge and eventually confront the fears you developed from your upbringing and societal influences. Changing your attitude can produce a new you:

From	**To**
"I will be a bag lady."	"I will have more than enough income each month."
"I will have to eat cat food."	"I will have enough food to share with others."
"I don't know where I will live."	"I will always live in a comfortable and warm home."
"I will have no money, and no one will come to see me."	"I will always be surrounded by people who want to spend time with me."
"I can't afford to send my kids to college."	"My kids will go to whatever school they choose."

By writing down your fears, you can create their opposite. *Write yours down now.* Put them in letters to yourself. Put them on Post-its, and put these reminders in places that you normally see throughout the day—on the mirror in your bathroom, on the refrigerator door, on your desk or work area, on the telephone handle. By writing down the old and creating the new, you birth a new script for your life.

SUMMING UP—WHAT WOMEN WANT

So what do women want? What do you want? The answers come from thousands of women I have met over the past year at workshops and conferences. They can be summarized as the 10 "S's."

Security

Women are concerned about their security—not just the physical, but the fiscal. What is going on with Social Security and Medicare? Can Congress be trusted to sort out the issues and set a realistic plan in motion in time to avoid a crisis? Many women today feel a vertical squeeze—financial and emotional responsibilities for kids (sons and daughters don't move out as soon as they did in previous generations) and parents (their mothers outlive their fathers and need or require financial and emotional support).

Safety

Wherever their money has been placed for preservation or growth, women want to know that a company or financial institution is not going to go out of business. When a woman invests her money, she wants to be secure with the notion that the individual she works with or places the money with for investment will react or behave in a stable manner. Will my money be safe? Will it be accessible? Will I be able to sleep at night?

Solvency

If Social Security converts to a form of private fund, will it be solvent? Will the dollar of today keep up with inflation tomorrow? Will my moneys have *real* value tomorrow, next year, when I retire?

Simplicity

Today's lifestyles come in sound bites. Everything is quick and fast. The speed doesn't allow for complexity. In reality, women have led the way for a more informal style of living over the past two decades. They want their money management in the same mode: no frills, just explanations of the pros and cons in easy-to-understand terms.

Strategies

With the incredible success of the stock market in the 1990s, women who invested in stock discovered that most of their decisions and any strategies they had resulted in profits. With the new millennium, will the stock market yield the same type of returns? Who knows? No one has a crystal ball. The Smart Money Woman wants to know what strategies will fit with her lifestyle as well as her overall objectives.

Because we know that women tend to live longer than men, whatever we elect to do must build toward our becoming self-reliant in money decisions. What options are there? Will there be an investment fad, or will there be something that if implemented today will be viable and successful when we retire? Will tomorrow's investment market be as successful as yesterday's?

Stewardship

Women feel responsible for what their moneys do—environmentally and communitywise. Women believe in the Momism that what goes around comes around. We women don't want to "kiss off" dollars; we want to know that our funds "do good"—for ourselves, our families, and our communities.

Solutions

Answers, simply answers. Women are bombarded on a daily basis with problems—their own, their families', the country's, even the world's—an almost overwhelming number. Women must learn to weed out the problems—theirs and others—that they have little or no input into or control over. Instead, women need to be creative and start working on the solution side of the ledger. Mistakes will be made, but at least that's movement, not paralysis via procrastination and politics.

Smarts

Let's give credit, lots of it, when it is due. Men are known for jumping into things and trying to solve whatever the problem is. We can do that too, though our methods may just be a little different. As women acquire knowledge in the money realm, our individual achievements will be amazing!

Satisfaction

Women want to feel that there is a reason, a rationale for whatever they do with their money. Women want satisfaction in what they do to earn their moneys, and they want to be satisfied that they have had multiple options to choose from. Success with money brings satisfaction. When women are satisfied that their overall strategies are right for them and their families, their sense of how they did their jobs sounds a bravo to their money-management skills. Women have traditionally not been encouraged to openly cheer their success. Internally, the Smart Money Woman knows that she is on track and tells herself, "You do good work."

Sense

Above all, women want to feel that whatever strategies they create and follow make sense for who they are and what they believe in. It's not enough to have money. The real question is "Am I comfortable with how I accumulate it, how I invest it, and what I do with it?"

There will always be some fear. Cartoon character Pogo said it best: "I have seen the enemy and the enemy is us." By bringing up your awareness level, by identifying which fears influence your money decisions, you will achieve the first level of smart money.

10 SMART MONEY MOVES TO REMOVE FINANCIAL FEARS FROM YOUR LIFE

1. **Enroll in a mini or short class taught at your local community college by a financial professional.** Be aware that most of these classes are presented by individuals as part of their marketing efforts—they hope to get you as a new client. Your initial goal in attending the class is to learn—the jargon, strategies, and investment options. You are never under any obligation to become a client.

2. **Start an investment club with some of your friends.** It's a great way to learn about stocks with a minimal dollar commitment (anywhere from $20 a month and up) and have fun.

3. **Review where you've spent money this past month.** Did you spend any money in a way that you now feel was a mistake or for items that really could have waited? Did you feel stupid? Or did you learn something—as in, "I won't waste money *that* way again."

4. **If you have kids over age six, plan a monthly money powwow and talk about what items your family "needs" versus just "wants" and how much they cost.** Your objective is to get discussions about money on the table.

5. **Host a potluck dinner at your house with your friends.** Tell them that it will be a "Can you top this?" tale about the goofiest or stupidest thing that they have done with money. The objective is to sow the idea that no matter how bad it looked or seemed, each person survived the goof.

6. **Put on your thinking cap.** Do a little mental probing—when did you not follow your own beliefs or "gut feelings" and it turns out that you were right in the first place? Once you commit to learning about and using money more effectively, you'll find that your feelings and gut reactions are often right on target.

7. **Find out where your money goes.** In the next three months, keep track of where every dime lands. Include the frozen yogurt, magazines, and the three dollars you misplaced.

8. **Call your bank and ask your representative or someone in customer service how much money you would have in twenty years if you put $100 in a savings account that earned 3 percent per month every month.** Now, call a brokerage company, such as Charles Schwab & Co. (800-724-7526), and ask the same thing, but *change* the percent you will receive to what the average growth rate of a Morningstar-rated growth mutual-fund company in a top 20 percent ranking has been the past five years (as the percent of growth you will receive for the next twenty years). If you have access to the Internet, go to *www.morningstar.com* and identify a fund from the ones listed under growth. Which yields more—the 3 percent bank account or the nonguaranteed mutual fund?

9. **Think—have you ever put money into an investment and had it decline in value?** Why did it decline? Was the stock market down in general? Was the industry you invested in experiencing negative publicity? Was the company losing money or reporting poor earnings? Did the loss cost you anything besides money (loss of sleep, mistrust in whomever recommended that you invest the money, negative feeling about investing in general, etc.)?

10. **Remember a time that you were afraid to do an activity (any activity) because you didn't understand how to do it or how it worked, and you did it anyway, and it worked out well.** What did you learn—that you were just lucky? Or that sometimes you don't need to know everything there is to know to move ahead?

Bridge a Money Taboo–Talk About It!

2

Do you know how much your family's income was when you were growing up? How about today? If you are like most people, your answer is probably, "No" or "I can only guess." I know I didn't have that information, and still don't—and I'm over fifty years old! Sometimes I wonder if my father knew how much he made over the years.

Growing up, I really didn't understand what my father did for a living; he just went to work every day. I don't recall him ever doing work at home. My mother was a stay-at-homer, typical of her generation. I know that she and my father talked about business over their nightly Scotches and that she usually paid the bills and did the taxes.

My family moved around a lot. We always had an unlisted phone number and rarely spent money on entertainment or vacations. We just didn't go out. My brothers and I have concluded in our adult years that our parents were one step ahead of their creditors. All of us were clueless as to what money flowed through our household, a situation that still is not uncommon today.

YOUR MONEY PERSONA

You may ask, "What motivates *me* with my money decisions and habits?" To find out, take the Smart Money Personality Quiz that follows. Instructions for scoring and determining your style are included.

Smart Money Personality Quiz

1. Your Aunt Martha dies, leaving you her prized pearls and stocks that have a current market value of $50,000. You

   A. immediately take the stocks to a broker and sell them so that you can buy the things you really want, especially a new wardrobe to go with the pearls.
   B. get the stock certificates and place them and the pearls in a safe deposit box.
   C. do nothing.
   D. sell the stocks and buy shares in companies that you think will double in value within the next few years.
   E. donate the shares to WISH List, your favorite nonprofit organization.

2. Your best friend has just filed for bankruptcy. You

   A. already advised your friend to charge everything she could on her credit cards before she filed for the bankruptcy.
   B. know that it will never happen to you because you save a lot of the assets you get.
   C. know that no money problem will ever force you to do *that*.
   D. worry that it could someday happen to you.
   E. decide that you don't want to be around her as much as you have been in the past.

3. The bonus you were counting on is only half of what you expected. You

   A. decide that a shopping spree is in order to offset your disappointment.
   B. take back the new outfit you purchased the previous week.
   C. can't tell your spouse how much it is.
   D. call and see if you can get the deposit back on the new car you wanted.
   E. withdraw—from yourself and your friends.

4. To be financially comfortable, you

   A. have enough coming in; therefore, comfort is just a matter of going to work.
   B. need to increase your salary and have at least a million dollars in savings.

C. are not really sure what you need.

D. need to pay for everything in cash, including a new car and house.

E. are able to increase your donations to charity.

5. You've just received a credit card offer in the mail. You

A. apply for anything that comes along, knowing that you can meet your monthly payments.

B. consider it only if it has no annual fee.

C. toss it in the trash.

D. put it in a pile of mail to be looked at some other time.

E. would only consider applying for the card if it supports one of your causes.

6. The stock market keeps going up. You

A. borrow money to invest.

B. call your broker to cash out.

C. don't have a clue what "up" means.

D. sell half of your current stock holdings.

E. endow a chair at your alma mater with the increased value of your investments.

7. You are one of the winners in a lottery. Your share of the prize is $10,000,000. You

A. quit your job, order a great new chair to watch your new sixty-inch TV, invite twenty of your friends for two weeks in Hawaii on your nickel, and order your dream car.

B. select the annuity option for the rest of your life.

C. are shell-shocked and eventually decide to hire a money manager to take over.

D. let each member of your immediate family buy a special "something," then invest the rest.

E. change your name so no one will know of your good fortune.

8. Your accountant has advised you to get your financial records in order. You

A. have always used the shoe-box approach and see no reason to take the time to transfer everything onto the computer.

B. are in your glory; the challenge of the new computer program fits you to a T.

C. know you will get to it; that's why you save *everything* in a box somewhere in the basement.

D. like to keep track of all the warranties you have received over the years, including the tags you rip off merchandise.

E. ignore your accountant—that's his or her job to keep track of stuff.

9. When I think about a budget, my response is

A. budget, what's a budget?

B. it's a good thing.

C. it's never been a topic of conversation in my household.

D. I like to tinker with them, especially on the computer.

E. I take great pride in always living within my means.

10. I worry about money when

A. I don't; I'd rather think of ways to spend it.

B. I'm awake; it's constantly on my mind.

C. ever I read or hear about bad financial news or I'm in a crisis.

D. I'm not involved in other things that take my mind off it.

E. not often; there are other, more important things to worry about.

Scoring: The greatest number of a given letter will indicate your money persona. There are pros and cons to each style.

Spender

If you have mostly A's, your attitude is "What I have, I will spend." Budgets aren't in your vocabulary; you freely spend money on your friends and you're likely to have credit card debt, which can get you into trouble. The plus is that you aren't held back by money worries and that you are generous, sometimes overly generous. A *spender* is likely to be the one who reaches for the tab when dining out with friends, much to the chagrin of a spouse.

Keeper

B's indicate that you fit the common perception of a hoarder. It's difficult for you to spend anything on anybody, from yourself to the ones you love. The plus is that when financial chaos hits the general population, you don't have to worry about taking care of your family. The negative is that *keepers* often hold back more if times look tough, even when they have what most would view as plenty of money.

Dodger

A preference for C statements means that you will do just about anything to avoid a discussion about money, even if it is good news. Deep inside you feel that you just don't have the skills to handle it. The plus is that you are not obsessed about what money is doing.

Postponer

When it comes to money, anyone having mostly D statements is inclined to put off spending whenever possible, no matter how small the amount. Money concerns envelop your thoughts to the point that you can be obsessed with what you perceive as the lack of money, even when you have substantial savings. A *postponer* is not necessarily a *keeper,* although there are similarities. Postponers are willing to spend money as long as there is ample backup in savings and investments. *Keepers* don't want to spend, period.

Atoner

A high number of E responses indicates that you may be embarrassed about the money you have, you make, or that you come from. Most *atoners* live fairly uncomplicated and luxury-free lives. If unexpected money is received, it is not uncommon for an *atoner* to pass it on to a cause. A common attitude among them is that "I didn't have it before and all was fine; I don't need it now." *Atoners* will rarely replace household items and cars with newer models until they absolutely have to be replaced. Money is rarely wasted.

No matter what your money persona is, one style is not any better than another, even though each impacts what you do with money now and what you will do with it in the future. In reality, a little bit of each style can make sense at different times of your financial life.

Getting Out of the Loop

Most likely, money and having or not having it wasn't talked about when you grew up. And your upbringing influences attitudes and practices involving money. Most women grew up in homes that avoided discussions about money; mine was like that. Or there may have been talk about money in your home, but rarely a discussion about it. The Oppenheimer survey referred to earlier in the Introduction bears this out—the great majority of women, 85 percent, wish their families had spoken about money and investments.

> The majority of adult women today do not know the annual salary of their parents.

It is still not that uncommon for a married woman to not know the full status of her household finances, including the salary of her spouse. Most American families talk about crime, violence, sex, and the weather before they would broach the topic of money.

In my workshops, women report that "they feel out of the loop" when it comes to *really* talking about money. If you feel out of the loop, most likely you continue that practice of financial silence within your family, sometimes, to yourself. Your attitude may be "If I don't talk about it, it won't be a problem in my life." In reality, if you don't acknowledge the use—and misuse—of money, a problem is usually created. In the end, it becomes a monster.

Family Talks

Growing up, I vowed that I wouldn't do a series of things to my children, if I ever had them, that my parents had done to me. I bet you had a similar list of "nevers." Talking about money wasn't on my list. I didn't know that it should be. My teenaged son Frank changed that when we were on a ski vacation. Riding up the mountain in the chairlift with me, he asked if I made a lot of money. His best friend had told him that I did—because his parents had told him so.

My response was, "Yes—and no. It depends what month it is." I went on to explain that I received moneys through commissions, royalties, and speaking fees. I didn't get a regular paycheck as his friend's parents did. Sometimes I received big checks, sometimes I received no checks. That ski lift changed the way I spoke with my kids about money. I told myself that

I was not going to leave them out of the loop—they would hear about the good stuff and the not-so-good if it came my financial way. The question was how to best keep the dialogue going.

Within the month, I had an idea. My three kids were in the eleven- to fifteen-year-old age range. Knowing that they were very visually oriented, I did something that made a significant impression on them. It all started when my son told me that his best friend's parents had said that I made a lot of money. At the time I was a stockbroker with E.F. Hutton. And, yes, there were months when I did make a lot of money. There were also months when I didn't make enough to pay the mortgage.

I tapped into my kids' visual resources to make the impression I wanted. Every month that summer, I cashed my checks before depositing them. I told the cashier to give me nothing larger than a 100-dollar bill and that I wanted plenty of smaller bills too. When I got home with the cash, I gathered up all the bills that needed to be paid that month.

Once a month, I called a family powwow. I told them that I had cashed my checks so they could see what "a lot of money" looked like. They were impressed with the size of the stack of currency in front of them, especially the hundreds. "Wow," was their reaction to the first 100-dollar bill they had ever seen. Then we got down to business. I laid out the mortgage and car payment coupon books. Bills were laid out for utilities, phone, auto and life insurance, department stores, gasoline—you get the idea.

Next, I dealt out the bills from my "cashed checks" like a deck of cards. Each bill was covered with the requisite amount of cash—$1,800 to the mortgage, $150 to gas and electricity, $200 for life insurance, $200 for auto insurance, $300 for health insurance, $150 for gasoline, and so forth. My kids' eyes were wide with amazement when I finished. I said, "Well, there's my income, that's what I made this month. And, yes, I did make a lot of money. But notice how much smaller the pile of cash is." They learned a valuable lesson. I had brought a lot of money *in* the door that day, but it would go *out* the door just as quickly.

Most kids have no idea how much just the basics cost their parents each month. And my kids were no different. They couldn't believe that I had laid out several thousand dollars for the *needed* monthly expenses. And we hadn't yet allocated anything for groceries and allowances, not to mention money for "fun" things. With the leftover money, my kids were ready to party—a trip sounded good to them. I told them, "No, I don't know how much money I will make the next month, if any, and we will need money to pay all the bills *again* that we just went through."

As you know, paychecks are usually "after-tax" dollars. I told the kids that deductions had been taken from my checks for taxes. Their mouths dropped open when I told them that state, federal, and Social Security taxes had eaten up almost 40 percent of my gross pay—they had no idea that I had a tax bill to pay before I even got my check. And I really had a challenge explaining that FICA and Social Security are the same thing— why does one tax have two names?

One of the kids quickly picked up on the fact that not all taxes are deducted from my pay. "What other taxes do you have to pay, Mom?" I told them about real estate taxes, sales taxes, and special city and county assessments. They decided that being an adult may not be so cool.

Summer months have always been interesting when it comes to income. With few exceptions, there is minimal cash flow in my house. Often there is not enough money to cover the basic needs and to pay the monthly bills. With this simple exercise, my kids learned *why* a savings program was critical to us—we usually have to dip deep into savings so we can eat and keep our house. This was the first time that they really understood what I meant when I said, "We can't afford it this month"—and that this was, and always had been, a valid statement.

Now they believed me—because the next month funds were limited. The monthly inflow did not exceed the monthly outflow. At our family powwow, the necessity for a savings plan became quite evident. As one of the kids said, "It's a good thing we didn't go on a trip and spend all your money." Exactly right.

Remember, kids are very visual. Let them see where your money goes by piling it up on each bill you owe, or you can make a card for each bill (don't forget savings, charity, and church). This exercise will take your kids light years ahead in their understanding of why spending and savings plans are critical to the successful Smart Money family.

SUMMING UP—DELETING THE ULTIMATE TABOO

You may have grown up as I did. Money talks were nonexistent in your household. You are not alone; millions of women have been in your footsteps before you, and millions will follow. Break the taboo and speak up. You need to for yourself and for your family. There are resources galore to begin your journey. Programs are offered at YWCAs, community colleges, financial planning firms, banks, women's organizations, and the like. Books are published every year that explore a variety of aspects of the money maze.

Your upbringing may have totally excluded money talks. You may have been brought up with the philosophy that there will be someone to take care of you. You may believe that if you are too good at the money maze men will find you undesirable or threatening. You may believe that you can't have both a relationship and success.

> Your choice is to continue the legacy of your upbringing *or* to create a new one for yourself. Which one will you choose?

YOU AND YOUR PERSONALITY

Now, let's come back to you. When you took the *Smart Money Personality Quiz,* what was your money persona—were you a spender, keeper, dodger, postponer, or an atoner? Each one of the money personalities influences how you handle stress, success, and strategies with money.

---

10 SMART MONEY MOVES TO TALK ABOUT MONEY

1. **Ask a few of your coworkers or friends to create a Smart Money shopping group; make a list of needed items and then identify stores that sell them.** Compare prices and see how much money you can save.

2. **If you have a 401(k) plan or other type of retirement program at work, ask a few of your coworkers to brainstorm about the various options you can select for investing your money.**

3. **If your parents are still alive, ask them to roll back their life time clocks and review with you the way they handled and invested their money, and how those strategies worked out—or didn't.**

4. **Scan the magazines you read and look for articles and advertisements about new products being produced.** Tell a friend that this might be an investment opportunity and ask her what she thinks.

5. **If you are a *spender*, you'll spend money you don't have. Curtail charging anything for the next sixty days.** Then reevaluate whether you really needed whatever it was you were contemplating buying or charging. Did you *really* need it? Or did you just want it?

6. **If you are a *keeper*, it is difficult for you to spend any money on something that is not considered essential or critical. Take 5 percent of your next paycheck and buy a gift—for yourself, your spouse, or a friend.** Tell the recipient you are working on being a new money you— one that can give and one that can keep, save, or invest.

7. **If you are a *dodger*, you hate to talk about or do anything with money. Start talking money, a little at a time.** Try opening a conversation at the next gathering of friends, family, or coworkers with something that is topical, such as Social Security. It's a common concern for many—will it be available to the baby boomers? Ask your friends what they think and what they are doing for their retirement funding.

8. **If you are a *postponer*, you put things off.** If you need a computer, or to update to a new one, and have the money for it, you still don't buy it. Why? Because you figure it will be less expensive next year and you can buy it for half price? Ask a close friend or spouse to help you weigh the pros and cons of buying it today versus waiting until next year.

9. **If you are an *atoner*, you feel embarrassed about any money you have, much less talking about it. Decide to make a year-end donation to a favorite cause.** Instead of doing it anonymously, as you have done in the past, instruct the organization to use your name in a future fund-raising effort.

10. **Make a commitment to yourself and your family that you will discuss your money situation on a regular basis.** If you have kids, include them, and be willing to share good news as well as bad.

Create a Realistic Financial Plan . . . and Stick to It

3

Imagine it's Saturday night and you tune into the late evening news. Your local TV station has started its drum roll for the weekly lottery drawing. You've been following it all week since no winners have been declared for the past month. The pot is more than $10,000,000 and you have decided to take the plunge. You've bought ten tickets, all based on your friends' birth dates. As you watch each number's being revealed, you can't believe it. You hold a winning ticket! Now, what do you do? Here's what usually happens.

In a rare instance, the "luck of the draw" creates an instant millionaire and a "media darling for the day." It creates the get-rich-with-no-effort syndrome. The great odds are that you, newly crowned millionaire, will find your bank account empty within a few years. Why? Because your only plan was to buy the lottery ticket. If it was a winner, the only "plan" for the money was quitting a job; going to Disney World; buying a car, boat, or home. Maybe you never thought you had a chance, so why make a plan anyway?

When I worked exclusively with clients (rather than doing the speaking, writing, and consulting that I presently do), I found that the most successful individuals who were able to create an expanding savings and investment program were those who had a long-range plan. Sometimes the plan involved a mere $25 per month; at other times, greater amounts. The women and men who consistently created a plan and stuck to it by making a regular financial commitment had far greater amounts of money at the end of their money-accumulation journey than those who made six-figure incomes and had no plan.

When I think back to the thousands of people that I worked with, the most successful were school teachers! Why? Because they consistently directed moneys toward their tax-sheltered programs (usually annuities) as soon as they started teaching. It was not uncommon for them to have guaranteed incomes of $4,000 to $5,000 a month when they left their blackboards, sometimes more than what they were making in their full-time employment.

> Putting together a plan requires some background—background on your spending habits, your dreams, and druthers—and an understanding of what money is.

The creation of a total financial plan has multiple components. Before you plunge into any type of investments, there are a variety of things you must do to protect yourself and those you care for and support. This Smart Money Move is a big one. I suggest you have highlighter, Post-its, paper, and pencil in hand as you go through this chapter.

THE "B" WORD

Just about everyone cringes when they hear the "B" word—budget. It's like a diet, not a lot of fun and sure to have restrictions. Let's rename budgets and call them *spending plans*. Spending plans usually address problem areas (where cutbacks are needed) and they allocate money to be spent. They also include plans for saving and investing.

In your Smart Money Move #4, "Tithe to Yourself," you will start to track where your money goes. You may find some surprises. As you sleuth, the most likely areas that you will find problems in—also known as overspending—will be money spent in fast-food and regular restaurants, and spent on convenience foods, entertainment, clothing, gifts and cards, vacations (once you are there, credit cards get maxed), and cash taken from the ATM.

> When you focus on "needs" rather than "wants," you stay in balance.

Your Recipe for a Smart Money Financial Plan

Today's financial plan has multiple components. They include:

- A detailed form, which you complete, that reveals much of the information needed in the points below. In addition, it queries you about your personal goals and aspirations. In your interviews, the planner will seek to ascertain what type of risks you can take, if any, in reaching your goals.
- An analysis of your spending and implementation of a realistic spending plan. This takes a magnifying glass to both your sources of income and your spending, saving, and investing habits.
- An analysis of your net worth. Anything that is considered an asset, whether there is a possibility of growth or not, will be included and analyzed. This serves as a benchmark or measurement of how far you have come and as a new starting line for where you are going.
- An analysis of your present retirement and pension plans. If you have none, specific recommendations will be made on where and how to get started.
- An analysis of what your present life insurance coverage is and what your present and anticipated needs are, plus recommendations for any changes. Some plans cover other types of coverage, including disability and long-term health recommendations.
- A current will or living trust in place. No financial plan is complete without one. Since few financial planners hold law degrees, yours will most likely refer you to a lawyer who specializes in wills and trusts, if you don't already have one.
- Recommended investments, which will most likely be needed. Over a period of time, you will use several types—stocks, mutual funds, and bonds will be the most common, but there's quite an arsenal to choose from. The advisor you choose to work with should identify the ones that fit your personal goals and needs.
- Payouts—what you should get at the end of your financial rainbow. Since no one can guarantee exactly what a potential investment or the plan that you decide on will do, a major portion of this section is a projection, based on historical performances of what is recommended.

Before the big sleuth, look in the mirror. Look around you. Of all the items in your house, which are necessities and which are just nice to have?

- Take an **inventory** in your house of all the items you routinely buy at the store and replace when used. Look in the bathrooms, kitchen, garage, yard—everywhere. Don't forget magazines, newspapers, and fresh flowers.
- On a piece of paper, make two columns: **Wants** and **Needs**.
- If there are multiple members in the household, have each write down in either of the columns what he or she believes each item to be. This assumes the family members are old enough to understand what a "want" or "need" is—wants being a soda, not a glass of water, for example.
- Compare lists. Restocking or purchasing the **Needs** should become the first order when money is available. **Wants** can be deferred, even eliminated, if they don't fit your goals.

You've already identified your sources of income. You are in the process of identifying where all your money goes each month. You have just tallied up the items that are necessities and those that are or would be nice to have. You are now ready to write a *spending plan,* a.k.a. budget.

Do you have more than enough money to cover your monthly obligations or not enough? Either way, probe your spending habits—your fixed and discretionary ones. When you set goals, prioritizing is essential. Until you feel that you have a true handle on spending, ask yourself, do I/we need this or do I/we want it? If the item doesn't fit into your goal plan, don't buy it. My advice may be harsh, but it's the only way to stop the "want" spending.

The Plan Is to Plan

So, how do you put together a viable financial plan? Financial plans belong in every woman's life. It doesn't matter if you have lots of money or are barely scratching by. Both scenarios have lots in common.

Let's say you have money—in fact, a *huge* amount of money. You may be tempted to take that long-awaited vacation cruise. A reward for all your hard work, for enduring the stress levels you've had to bear the past year in regard to a settlement in a suit, an inheritance, or even for getting through a divorce. Take Sarah. She shared her saga when she first came to my office.

SMART MONEY MONTHLY
SPENDING PLAN

Fixed Expenses

These are payments for the same amount paid monthly:

Car   Retirement accounts

Insurance   Savings

Loans   Taxes

Mortgage or rent

A Total: Fixed expenses

Flexible Expenses

These are necessities that vary monthly and annually:

Food   Laundry/dry cleaning/cleaning

Charity/church   Personal grooming

Clothing   Transportation (other than your car)

Health care not   Other
   covered by insurance

Investing

B Total: Flexible expenses

Discretionary Spending

These are all the things you "want":

Eating out   Vacations

Entertainment   Other

Gifts

C Total: Discretionary spending

D Total (A + B + C = D) of all spending:

E Total income sources from Smart Money Move #3:

F Amount of income over or <under> spending (E – D = F):

When I got divorced three years ago, I got a check for $656,000 in return for no alimony. I thought I had won the lottery—I had never seen so much money! Since then, I have traveled, bought jewelry, and a new car, and loaned and given money to friends. I had a great time. I didn't buy a house because I figured I could do that after I stopped traveling. I even took several friends on an around-the-world cruise for two months. I've had a wonderful time but my money runs out next month—*what do I do?*

For starters, Sarah should have done some planning when she first got her money. She didn't, and blew it. She could have been set for life—$656,000 is a lot of money, money that could have given her a nice trip or two or, better yet, it could have seeded multiple investments that would have created income and growth. This scenario is a modern-day tragedy that is repeated more often with women than with men.

WHAT'S NEXT?

You've identified your *needs* and *wants,* committed to creating a viable spending plan, determined what things are really increasing or decreasing that you routinely buy, and gained a better understanding of what inflation and deflation do to your dollar. So what should be your next step? Unless you are well versed in the myriad choices available to you, start by talking to a financial planner, preferably a certified financial planner.

You start by figuring out what your assets and your liabilities are. If you haven't already done so, it's time to complete your inventory of personal assets. If you have completed a loan application, you are familiar with assets and liabilities.

YOUR NET WORTH—THE TOOL FOR MEASUREMENT

One of your first steps in developing your Smart Money profile is to determine what your net worth is. It will become the baseline for checking your pulse on how you are doing. You figure this by adding up your assets and subtracting your debts and liabilities. The result is your net worth.

Ideally, your assets are of greater value than your liabilities. If they aren't, don't give up. You, and your family, will always be the single best asset you have. It will be your ability and efforts that will create your future net worth. Your material assets may be on the lean side today; next year, the

SMART MONEY NET WORTH STATEMENT

Assets—What You Own

Bank accounts
- Checking   _____
- Savings, CDs   _____

Deposits

Money market accounts   _____

Insurance cash values   _____

Bonds   _____

Investments
- Mutual funds   _____
- Stocks   _____
- Rental property   _____

Retirement plans   _____

Home   _____

Cars   _____

Antiques, artwork, jewelry   _____

Personal property   _____

Other   _____

Total Assets (add all of the above assets)   _____

Liabilities—What You Owe

Credit cards   _____

Mortgage(s)   _____

Car loans   _____

Student loans   _____

Other debts   _____

Total Liabilities (add all of the above liabilities) _____

Net Worth (total assets minus total liabilities) _____

picture can be totally different. The deciding factor will depend on what
you do from this day forward.

There are two components to your net worth: the material side—assets
minus liabilities—and the emotional side. It's usually straightforward to
gauge the material side; the emotional side carries components that are
more difficult, if not impossible, to weigh. Between spouses and within
families it is not uncommon to find risk-taking attitudes and abilities on
the opposite end of the spectrum.

What may be fine and comfortable for you as an investment option
may give your spouse nightmares. The key is to identify these differences
and discuss them openly. There may very well be some areas that should
be avoided when it comes to investments. You and your spouse need to
determine if any fears or concerns are valid, and if they are, you can mod-
ify your plan to both your satisfactions.

The only way to create a net worth statement is to do one. You can
copy one from the zillions of financial planning and money workbooks
in bookstores today; you can get a blank loan application; or you can
use the *Smart Money Net Worth Statement*. Whichever method you
choose, the important thing is to do it now. Most of the information
that you need to fill in the blanks you have gathered during the preceding days.

You will need to know the values of any investments and retirement
plans that you own and participate in. Don't use the new car value for
cars—figure a minimum reduction of 20 percent of the value when you
drive off the lot. Investments, art, antiques, and jewelry values are what
you can get for them if you sold today. Take the latest statement values for
bank, savings, and any insurance accounts. Your home's value is what you
could sell it for today, not what you bought it for. Your various debt balances would be what the account balances would be if you paid off now
versus at the later date you contracted for.

When you have determined your net worth, ask yourself these questions:

- Do I need more money now to supplement my current income?
- Do I now know where I have kissed off dollars on a regular basis?
- Do I need to pay off any debt (which would use up some of my assets)?
- Do I want to buy a house or put money in something that will
  reposition liquid assets to an illiquid asset? (Liquid assets are those
  you can get the money or cash for within a few days; illiquid assets
  are the opposite—it could take months, even years to access the
  money.)

- Am I concerned about retirement? Do I want to make my funds grow as fast as possible?
- Am I saving or investing any money on a regular basis?
- Have I guesstimated what my tax obligation will be for the year and made any adjustments to my W-4 so that I don't get a refund?
- Am I now talking about money more positively, to myself and to my family?
- Am I ready to commit some of my time and energy to become a Smart Money Woman now?

The mere fact that you have read this far in this book shows that you are willing to commit to moving forward through the money maze. Answering yes to at least three of the previous questions indicates that you probably are ready to create a plan—a plan that will be altered at times when your specific circumstances demand it.

DURABLE POWER OF ATTORNEY

Do not skip this section. *Every woman and man should have a durable power of attorney*—a legal instrument that tells adults who may have to step in on your behalf what you want. Powers of attorney are needed for the unexpected—accidents, life-threatening illnesses, paralyzing strokes, and weird events that can occur in society that no one wants to happen to them and their loved ones. But they do happen, and they happen every day.

Consider the news in my morning paper—it's a heartbreaking story of a young mother who went to the hospital to give birth to her second son. Normally a joyous event, this one turned into a family feud.

The mother experienced an extremely rare blood problem at the birth and went into a coma after the doctors pumped over three times her normal blood amount into her via transfusions. The woman went from a critical to a vegetative state in a fairly short period of time. Enter the family. The husband was in shock. They had been married less than a year. He kept praying for a miracle and wanted to keep her alive. Her sisters wanted to pull the plugs and cease tube-feeding her. Eventually the court was involved. The woman was only forty years old. She died after eight months of being kept alive.

So, what happens to you if something happens to you?

What should you do to protect your interests? First of all, determine who you truly trust, someone who will act as your "voice" in an emergency—a backup if you can't function, are in an accident, or become very ill suddenly. This person can be your spouse, friend, adult child, or a parent. Talk to her or him about the unexpected. I promise you, the individual won't relish your discussion, but it's one that you will never regret initiating. Tell the person what you want done if you become incapacitated in any way. If he or she is willing, give the individual your power of attorney now—in writing. Your age doesn't matter—everyone needs a backup.

HEALTH CARE

For health care, you need a special form, which varies from state to state. You can drop by any hospital and pick up a health-care durable power of attorney packet that's right for your state. Or you can write to Choice in Dying, 200 Varick Street, Tenth Floor, New York, NY 10014-4810 or call 800-989-9455 for a packet for your state to be sent to you. It's free.

It's a good idea to name two stand-ins for you in case one might not be around if an accident occurs and a critical decision has to be made. To avoid any inaction or delay, either one should be able to act alone. Make sure your personal physician, spouse, and family members know what your druthers are.

FINANCIAL

If you aren't sure what you want done in the event that you become incapacitated, you can create a *springing power of attorney*. It only comes to life if you become disabled and can't act for yourself. Your springing power of attorney will define what that means. It will read something like this:

> *I shall be deemed disabled when two physicians licensed to practice medicine in my state sign a document stating that I am disabled and unable to handle my personal affairs. If this happens, then Sheryl Briles will handle my affairs. When two physicians licensed to practice medicine in my state sign a document stating that I am able to handle my affairs again, Sheryl Briles will no longer serve as my power of attorney.*

Durable powers of attorney are another form of insurance, and they should be reviewed every four to five years. If you decide that you want to change yours, including the person who would act on your behalf, it's a good idea to inform the individual, both verbally and in writing. Destroy whatever copies you had made previously and substitute new ones.

NEXT ON YOUR AGENDA

If you told me, "I want my investments to create *extra income* for me while they *grow fast,* and I want them to be *really safe,*" my response would be, "Forget it. You are asking the impossible. You may be able to find a blend of two out of the three but not all three."

If you have not interviewed and secured the services of a financial planner, now's the time to do so. At this point, you have accumulated the information that this professional needs to assist you in developing a plan that is designed for you. One of the plusses of using a planner, at least during a structuring or restructuring of your money strategy, is that this person stays current as to what is available on the market in the area of insurance and investments; what the tax ramifications (and benefits) are; what your present tax obligations are, and what if any beneficial adjustments could be made; and how best to maximize the use of pension and deferred compensation plans. Also, a financial planner will make inquiries about wills and trusts, referring you to an attorney who will update or create one if appropriate.

> Your financial planner will most likely act as pilot of your money ship. You, though, are not relegated to water-girl duty. You are copilot and must never leave the bridge. Your responsibilities don't stop at knowing where your money goes or what investments you have.

Every plan requires a review of what kind of insurance you have. For the sake of space, I'm going to concentrate on the area of life insurance. When you first talk to an agent or financial planner, it seems like there are an incredible variety of life insurance products. Granted, there are lots of names, but there are really only a few basic flavors.

INSURANCE: WHO, WHAT, AND HOW

The only people for whom life insurance is useful are those whom you leave behind when you die. The question is not "if"—you will! The question is "when?" Life insurance is not for you—it's for the people in your life who depend on you financially. Unless you want to leave a special bequest for a charity, or will have estate taxes, *do not* buy any life insurance if no one is financially dependent on you. Having the right kind of insurance, particularly life insurance, is one of your Smart Money Moves. [Some of the material in this section originally appeared in my book *Money Sense* (Moody Press), which was published in 1994 and is no longer in print.]

> There are three reasons why you buy life insurance:
>
> 1. To replace income if you die prematurely and family members depend on that income.
> 2. To provide money to buy out a business partner, repay business loans, or hire a successor in case of an owner's death.
> 3. To provide immediate, liquid money to pay estate taxes.

As you begin to probe the maze that is insurance land—and believe me, it is—keep two rules in mind:

- *Keep it simple.* It is easy to go brain-numb when considering insurance. If you really don't understand the concept of what an agent is proposing, take a pass.
- *Frugality wins.* Buy the lowest cost insurance you can. Stretching your dollar to get the most for the least is your guiding principle.

Life insurance is death protection—protection for those you love and care for. Other types of insurance that go beyond pure death protection, with savings and investments attached to the policy as part of the deal, have a hefty price tag attached. More on that later.

WHO NEEDS INSURANCE?

Not everyone. But, maybe you. Below are several scenarios. See if you fit any of them:

1. *You're young, single, with no dependents.* Stop here—you don't need it. Instead, purchase disability coverage, add to your investments, and aggressively seed your retirement account.

Insurance agents who advise you to buy cash-value coverage because premiums are lower when you are younger are not your friends. If you don't need insurance, you'd be wasting your money. It's like buying scuba diving equipment just in case you might want to take up the sport ten years from now.

Agents usually make the pitch that it's less costly now to buy a whole-life (versus a term) policy and you start saving right away. Here are the facts: the difference between buying a term policy at age thirty versus age forty is about $27 per year. That's not a big deal. What the agent didn't tell you was that a commission (often the entire first year's premiums on whole life) was paid. Term policies don't pay much to the agent.

Smart Money Move. Skip insurance and invest the amount you would have paid in premiums in a mutual fund.

2. *You're older, single, with no dependents.* You don't need life insurance. If you have some, does it have any cash value? And what interest rate does it earn? Most likely, you can earn more in your bank—and you can use it.

    Smart Money Move. Cancel insurance and use any accumulated cash to invest, put in savings, or live on.

3. *You're single with dependents.* Dependents come in all ages: babies to elderly parents. Insurance alert! What happens if you die tomorrow? If you are divorced and you have children, the kids may go to their father. Would he need to pay for child care, housekeeping, and other such services if you weren't there? If so, a term policy of $100,000 plus on your life makes sense. What about the elderly parents? Who will provide care and supplement their income? A policy makes sense.

    If you have children from a prior marriage, it can get complicated when it comes to money. A life insurance policy could be placed in a trust that would designate disbursements—your lawyer, agent, or financial planner will help here (after you tell them what you want).

    If relatives will become guardians, do your kids *and their potential guardians* a huge favor by having insurance proceeds to fund education needs.

    Smart Money Move. If you are under fifty years of age and a nonsmoker, you can get a term insurance policy for less than $200 a year—that's $16 per month!

4. You're a DINK—*a double-income couple with no kids.* You might not need insurance. Each spouse could be self-supporting if the other dies. Buy coverage only if you need both incomes to cover obligations (don't forget the mortgage). If you each have an estate valued at over $650,000, you may need cash to pay taxes.

   Smart Money Move. Because of changes in the workforce today, it is critical to build your liquidity moneys—moneys you can access within seven days. DINKS spend money—lots of it! Look at spending, cut down on eating out, and invest the difference.

5. You're an OINK—*a one-income couple with no kids.* The working spouse needs insurance to protect and preserve the lifestyle of the spouse at home.

   Smart Money Move. If the spouse at home has independent moneys, pass on life insurance. If not, insurance is needed to cover obligations that were created because of the other spouse's earning ability. When figuring out what you need, include the entire mortgage balance.

6. *You're married, with young children.* You need insurance, lots of it. Those kids have to be raised and educated, and that's not cheap.

   Smart Money Move. Get out your checkbook. You should allow six to seven times your annual earnings to take care of your family. But you probably need the coverage only until they're on their own. Then this portion of your insurance can be canceled. Let's hear that applause for the income boost you feel after the kids go on their own.

7. *You're married and don't work for pay.* If you don't have children, pass on getting insurance on your life. Your spouse should be covered in case of his death. If you have small children, would your husband need to pay for housekeeping and child-care services? If so, you may need an insurance policy.

   Smart Money Move. If your marriage assets haven't accumulated large sums of cash and investments, your spouse may not have the extra income to cover child-related expenses. Remember, if you are under age fifty, a term policy costs less than $200 per year for $100,000 in coverage. Get it.

8. *You're retired or close to it.* You need insurance only if your spouse couldn't live on the Social Security, pension, and savings you'll leave behind. If your spouse dies, cancel your insurance. Keep it only if you have plenty of money to live on and want to leave a big check for your church, charity, or your kids, or if your estate will owe taxes.

Smart Money Move. The media are full of stories about the problems facing Social Security. Will it be there for you? The answer is yes. Will it have some changes to it? The most likely answer again is yes. Will it be drastically cut? I don't think so. As of 1997 the average retirement benefit for all Social Security retirees was $745 per month. To determine where you currently stand, call 800-772-1213 and ask for the Request for Personal Earnings and Benefit Estimate Statement (Form 7004).

It's a good idea to check up on it every three years to make sure that no errors have been added to your profile and that any current earnings are being credited. You can also tap into the Internet address for the Social Security Administration and request Form 7004. Go to *www.ssa.gov.*

9. *You're a kid.* Pass unless you are a movie star or you have a genetic disorder that will make insurance coverage unattainable when you become an adult.

Smart Money Move. If you have a policy bought for you as a child by your great-grandmother, cash it in. The bank will pay a higher savings interest than the insurance company will.

> In planning for college, invest in a no-load mutual fund. As your money grows, add several funds. Do not buy life insurance to fund educational costs. Parents and grandparents routinely are sold these policies—pass, pass, pass!

10. *You're a college student.* This is a waste of money for you, too—no dependents. You might feel guilty and think this is a way to pay your folks back? Pass.

Smart Money Move. Just say no.

11. *You own a business.* Either you or the company should have a policy on your life. You may need to cover the debts the company representatives signed personally for or to pay estate taxes. A co-owner may want to be able to buy his or her partner's share of the business if the partner dies or becomes disabled. Talk to your lawyer about a buy/sell agreement that is funded by life and disability insurance. This is known as "key man" insurance.

Smart Money Move. Don't trust that your partner(s) will take care of your spouse and kids when you are gone. Your family may own a percentage of the business, but if the company doesn't make any cash distributions, it's difficult to eat paper.

12. *You are self-employed or own a business and have kids.* When you are the person who creates "your" paycheck and something happens that would impair your work ability, you may not get paid. If you work for yourself and tragedy hits your home, how well can you function?

When my nineteen-year-old was killed in an accident, I was nonfunctional for many months. I forgot to pay the phone and utility bills—our utilities were turned off. I couldn't even remember to pay the mortgage payment! Because I was nonfunctional, I didn't make much money. If I didn't make money, bills and paychecks didn't get paid. When you work for someone else, coworkers cover for you and your paycheck continues.

Smart Money Move. Buy a $100,000 term insurance policy on each of your kids. The cost will be approximately $100 per year. If there is a death, you will have these funds that will allow you to grieve—to take some time off, to get counseling if needed, and to heal. When you are self-employed, that luxury isn't yours unless you have a big bank account to back you up.

13. *Your job (or your spouse's) pays into Social Security.* When Social Security was started in the 1930s, no one foresaw that kids would be covered. Guess what—those under age nineteen are when a parent dies. Here's more: Social Security will pay an income to

- a surviving spouse age sixty and up.
- a disabled spouse age fifty and up.
- a spouse who remarries a Social Security recipient. She can still collect on the first spouse's account if it pays more.
- a surviving spouse (who hasn't remarried) caring for a child under age sixteen or one who was disabled before age twenty-two.
- unmarried dependent children under age eighteen.
- unmarried dependent children under age nineteen if they are still in secondary school.
- parents at least sixty-two years and older who had been getting at least half their support from the worker who died. Don't forget— there's a lump-sum death benefit of $255 to the surviving spouse.

Smart Money Move. Make sure you check all your possible sources of retirement funds, including Social Security.

14. *You're rich.* You may need money to pay estate taxes. If your investments are illiquid (real estate and privately owned companies fit here), you need money—ready cash.

    Smart Money Move. If you're in this category, ideally you should have set up an irrevocable trust to keep the insurance proceeds out of your estate.

15. *You are getting divorced and will receive alimony or child support or have moneys still due you when the divorce is final.* With the purchase of an insurance policy on your ex's life for the amount(s) owed, you'll have an extra safety net if your ex owes you money for any reason.

    Smart Money Move. Purchase a policy (usually term insurance) on your ex's life and keep it in force for as long as moneys are due you. You are the owner and you pay the premiums. If you are in the process of a divorce, this can be included as part of the settlement agreement.

16. *Someone owes you money.* At some time you may loan money to a friend or family member. I don't mean a few hundred dollars; I'm talking thousands. What happens if your friend dies? Do you think her family will rush in with their checkbooks to pay you back? Probably not.

    Smart Money Move. Purchase a policy on your friend for an amount closest to the nearest $5,000. If you loaned your friend $8,000, buy a $10,000 policy. You pay the premium and own it. Once the loan is paid, cancel the policy.

WHAT'S WHAT IN INSURANCE

There are two types of insurance and a zillion hybrids. *Term* and *whole-life* insurance are the most common. *Universal life* was introduced several years ago, which sort of combined the two—and then there are variations of each. You may come across fixed or flexible premium, fixed or variable, one-insured or multiple-insured, first-to-die, second-to-die, and even blended policies. All of them start from either a term or whole life component. Anything outside of straight term or whole life will be a hybrid of the two. Some policies pay big commissions to agents, others very little.

Term insurance answers most needs when it comes to replacing lost income. These are the key parts of a term insurance policy:

- You pay premiums every year (monthly, quarterly, or annually). The insurance policy stays in force until you stop paying the premiums. There is no cash buildup—no savings.

- With ordinary term insurance, your premium increases slightly each year. You can buy a level term, however, which keeps the premium fixed for several years, then increases.

- Costs are determined by age, whether you smoke (if you haven't smoked for two years, you are considered weed-free), and gender (although some insurance companies have unisex rates).

- Companies vary in what they charge—the same policy and amount of coverage can cost twice as much at another company.

- The policy should be renewable—which means you don't have to requalify by having a physical every year, as long as you pay the premiums on time.

Whole-life insurance has a savings account attached to it. The longer you are in it, the more savings you will have. In order to achieve this, whole-life's premiums are much greater than term's in the early years of the policy. When whole-life is proposed, it is always accompanied by illustrations—the "what-ifs." Projections for growth in the savings side are *always* inflated—and they are *never guaranteed!*

It's easy to be misled on interest rates. Insurance companies routinely announce high interest rates to keep policyholders at bay; then they increase their operating expenses and charges for mortality (the death benefit). These expenses are deducted from your cash value before any interest is paid.

The result is that you do get a higher interest rate, but it's paid on a smaller amount of cash. You earn less, therefore, than the promised rate.

Universal-life insurance offers some flexibility. You can ascertain a guaranteed policy amount for when you die; you can accumulate tax-deferred cash; you can pay extra premiums early on, so that extra cash will build up (theoretically) and so that your extra cash will pay future premiums. Here's the catch: if the interest or investment rates projected in your illustration are not achieved (after all, rates do vary), you may have a problem—your cash won't build up to pay the premiums down the road.

If you select a universal-life policy, I would encourage you to go with one that does not have the fixed-interest option. Why? Many of these were sold when interest rates were higher; projections for accumulated interest haven't panned out. Overall, the stock market has outperformed the interest-related markets for growth. The policy you should look at is the *variable universal life*. Its performance is based on the success of the mutual fund that the insurance company manages. Today, there is enough actual history of performance for you to be able to compare apples with apples (versus apples with who knows what).

PAY THE PIPER

How much should you pay for life insurance? The amount you pay each year is called a *premium*. After you decide how much life insurance you need in your particular situation, the amount of your annual premium is based on four calculations:

- your age;
- your current state of health;
- how much money the insurance company can earn by investing your premium dollars until you die; and
- the insurance company's expenses for paying the agent commissions and sending you bills and statements.

HOW MUCH CHEAPER IS TERM INSURANCE?

Selected from lower-cost companies, the table of yearly premiums shows dramatically how much more coverage you get for your money with term insurance. The premiums quoted are for a $100,000 policy for a non-smoking male. Premiums for women will cost less. The term premiums rise every year; those for cash-value policies can stay level for life. But in terms of what's affordable at any given age, term insurance wins hands down. Remember, there are no savings or investment plans with straight term; that comes with the other types. The only way you will outdo your whole-life counterparts is to invest the difference continually, such as with a mutual fund. If you don't, thirty years down the road your whole life or its brethren will be sitting with several hundred thousand dollars.

Yearly Premiums for a $100,000 Policy

Age	Term insurance	Universal-life insurance	Whole-life insurance
30	$136	$ 590	$ 875
35	140	746	1,095
40	163	950	1,391
45	205	1,217	1,776
50	320	1,583	2,311
55	440	2,078	3,038
60	610	2,741	4,717
65	980	3,665	5,376

Source: National Insurance Consumer Organization.

HOW TO FIND CHEAP INSURANCE

There are two ways to find the companies that might mean lower insurance costs to you.

NICO

First check with the National Insurance Consumer Organization (NICO). In early 1991 NICO set out the following *maximum* rates that consumers might be charged for annual renewable term insurance. If your coverage costs more, it's too expensive. Write NICO at

National Insurance Consumer Organization
121 N. Payne St.
Alexandria, VA 22314

PRICE-QUOTE SERVICES

You can probably find lower rates than these NICO maximums, however, by checking with the insurance price-quote services. *To locate a computerized price-quote service* all the information you need is your age, gender, and health status; the computer starts to crunch information. It's a good idea to recheck every three to five years—who knows what "deals" will be out there. Following are some companies that offer insurance price-quote services.

There is no obligation to buy and no salesperson will call you to sell you a policy. In other words, you are in charge. Contact more than one; each may have different insurance companies in their computer banks of data.

- *Insurance Information* (800-472-5800). For $50, Insurance Information sends you the names and phone numbers of the five insurers that offer the lowest term rates for someone with your stats. Your $50 will be refunded if you don't find a policy more than $50 cheaper than the one you presently have. Insurance Information does not sell you insurance.

- *InsuranceQuote*
  800-972-1104
  www.iquote.com
- *Quote Smith*
  800-431-1147
  www.quotesmith.com
- *SelectQuote*
  800-343-1985
  www.selectquote.com
- *TermQuote*
  800-444-8376
  www.rcinet.com/~termquote
- *Wholesale Insurance Network*
  800-808-5810

Caution—price quotes are accompanied by brief descriptions (not with great details) of the policies. Make sure that you ask for *annual, renewable term* quotes. Many services will give a reentry or revertible term, which means you have to requalify in a few years (as with health insurance).

Groups that will connect or refer you to individuals who sell low-load or no-load policies are:

- *USAA;* 800-531-8000. A phone and mail service only, no agent shows up from USAA. Its representatives are all salaried, not on commission. USAA offers several types of term policies from convertible to no-commission cash-value policies.

- *Fee for Service;* 800-874-5662. This service will direct you to financial planners who sell low-load cash-value insurance. The fees for consultation or analysis of current policies run about $100 to $150 an hour. The company's policies typically come with a charge 20 percent less than the usual agent's commission for similar policies.

- *Life Insurance Advisors' Association (LIAA);* 800-521-4578. LIAA is a national association of fee-only advisors. Members' objectives are to offer unbiased life insurance; low-cost, noncommissioned insurance; and independent reviews of policies clients currently hold. Any policy the association recommends is not commission motivated—you will pay the advisor an independent fee. Remember, there is no free lunch.

As a guideline, the following is a table of rates supplied by NICO:

The Most You Should Pay for Term Insurance

Annual premium* (Nonsmokers)			*Annual premium* (Smokers)*		
Age	Male	Female	Age	Male	Female
18–30	$ .76	$ .68	18–30	$ 1.05	$ 1.01
31	.76	.69	31	1.10	1.05
32	.77	.70	32	1.15	1.10
33	.78	.71	33	1.21	1.15
34	.79	.72	34	1.28	1.20
35	.80	.74	35	1.35	1.25
36	.84	.78	36	1.45	1.31
37	.88	.82	37	1.56	1.38
38	.92	.86	38	1.68	1.45
39	.97	.90	39	1.81	1.52
40	1.03	.95	40	1.95	1.60
41	1.09	1.00	41	2.12	1.73
42	1.17	1.05	42	2.30	1.89
43	1.25	1.10	43	2.50	2.05
44	1.34	1.15	44	2.72	2.22

45	1.45	1.20	45	2.95	2.40
46	1.59	1.29	46	3.22	2.59
47	1.74	1.41	47	3.52	2.79
48	1.91	1.53	48	3.85	3.01
49	2.10	1.66	49	4.21	3.23
50	2.30	1.76	50	4.60	3.50
51	2.49	1.90	51	4.97	3.79
52	2.70	2.06	52	5.38	4.10
53	2.96	2.22	53	5.82	4.44
54	3.40	2.40	54	6.29	4.80
55	3.40	2.60	55	6.80	5.20
56	3.66	2.79	56	7.31	5.58
57	3.94	3.00	57	7.87	5.99
58	4.23	3.22	58	8.46	6.43
59	4.55	3.46	59	9.10	6.90
60	4.90	3.70	60	9.80	7.40
61	5.43	3.98	61	10.83	7.95
62	6.02	4.28	62	11.98	8.54
63	6.67	4.60	63	13.25	9.18
64	7.40	4.93	64	14.65	9.86
65	8.20	5.30	65	16.20	10.60

*Per $1,000 of coverage, per year.

Source: National Insurance Consumer Organization.

Notes:

- The table shows the premium rate per $1,000 of coverage. If you're buying a $100,000 policy, multiply the cost by 100 and add $60 (for the insurer's fixed policy expenses) to see the most that you should pay.
- Policies under $100,000 cost a little more per $1,000 of coverage; policies written for $500,000 and up cost a little less.
- Nonsmoker rates are for lessened health risks.
- The relative rates for smokers keep rising as insurers note how fast the smokers are dying.
- Rates and companies may have changed by the time you read this. For an update, check the latest NICO guide, *Taking the Bite Out of Insurance: How to Save Money on Life Insurance,* available at bookstores or by contacting NICO, 121 N. Payne St., Alexandria, VA 22314.

Buying Directly

One other way to cut out the middleman (agent) is to buy a no-load policy directly from the insurance company. No load means that you pay no commissions, which becomes attractive when whole-life or cash-value insurance is your choice. A few of the best direct sources are these:

- *Ameritas*—800-552-3553

    Individual representatives, not commissioned salespeople, of Ameritas Life Insurance respond to your questions. Ameritas offers other policies that are sold by agents, but to get the direct sales office you must use the toll-free number listed.
- *Southland*—800-872-7542 x6518

    Fee-based advisors and financial planners are affiliated with distributors of Southland's policies. Rates are very competitive.

One other useful resource is *The Individual Investor's Guide to Low-Load Insurance Products* by Glenn Daily. You can order it by calling International Publishing at 800-488-4149. The book costs $22.95 plus $2 shipping.

Who's the Fairest in the Land?

There are five companies who rate insurance companies: A.M. Best, Duff & Phelps, Moody's, Standard & Poor's, and Weiss Research. Most insurance companies quote their A.M. Best rating to answer queries about their safety and solvency. When Executive Life failed in 1991, A.M. Best was still rating the company "A+"! Go ahead and fake a yawn if you get the Best rating—what you want is the Weiss Research rating.

Weiss Research is the newest rating kid on the block—and the most conservative. Before Executive Life went belly up, Weiss's rating of it had been reduced to "D." To date, libraries don't carry Weiss. You can contact Weiss directly, however, and ask your rating questions. The ratings aren't free; your cost will be $15.

Agents won't tell you if the insurance company they are promoting is unsafe. Most of them don't know. Nor will they tell you that any investment projections are unrealistic. You may get a low quote for future premiums—whose price may depend on the company's making a 15 to 20 percent profit on its investment portfolio. Forget it. And it is a rare agent who will tell you that you can get a better deal someplace else. After all, why should he or she?

Rating Companies

A.M. Best—900-555-2378
Duff & Phelps—312-368-3100
Moody's—212-553-5377
Standard & Poor's—212-208-1527
Weiss Research—800-289-9222

DISABILITY INSURANCE

Disability insurance is usually treated with a benign approach. Ignore it and it will go away. It's an important coverage to include in your planning.

There are three general types of definitions or criteria that insurance companies use to determine the extent of the disability:

- Totally incapacitated and confined to bed
- Unable to work at any occupation
- Unable to work at a specific occupation

As a rule, the sooner benefits begin, the more costly the policy. On average, a person returns to work, whether from a critical illness or an accident, in twenty-one days. When you go disability policy–shopping, look at policies that commence in ninety days. The premium costs will be substantially reduced from a thirty-day wait policy.

The real question is how much do you need? If you pay for the policy yourself, any proceeds you receive from it will be nontaxable. If your employer pays for it, then all of the proceeds are taxable to you if you receive any benefits. If you pay and benefits are nontaxable, you should carry coverage of about 60 percent of your monthly income (if you make $3,000 a month, for example, $1,800 is 60 percent); if benefits are taxable, you need 80 to 90 percent of your income ($2,400 to $2,700 per month).

The next step is to check out what your savings and investments yield in interest and dividends. If you could qualify for Social Security disability benefits, what would you receive? If you had an injury at work, would Workmen's Compensation pay you benefits? Whatever all that tallies to, you then deduct the sum from the percent of your monthly income. If, after checking all your sources, you determine you could receive approximately $1,200 a month, the coverage you would seek would be $600 per month ($1,800 − $1,200 = $600).

Policy Needs

As with any contract, you can make or break it in the small print. Here's what to seek in a policy:

- It should contain a *noncancelable clause.* This means that as long as you keep paying the premiums, the insurance company can't cancel your policy, no matter what.
- It should have a *guaranteed annual premium clause,* which means that premiums cannot increase that have already been cited within the policy. As with buying life insurance, the younger you are, the less the policy will cost.
- You want it to have a *waiver of premiums clause* that guarantees that if you do become disabled, you no longer have to pay premiums to keep the policy in force.
- Ideally, your policy should have a *residual benefit disability payment.* This means that if you are disabled and eventually return to work, but at a lower rate, the insurance company will pay the difference between what you used to get from your employer with what your new rate is.

Finally, make sure that the wording in the policy states that it will pay for any disability caused by illness as well as by an accident.

Long-Term-Care Insurance

You will hear more and more about long-term-care insurance, or LTC. Your regular health insurance coverage does not include long-term care. None of them do. An LTC policy covers the unexpected, such as a stroke or disability that requires ongoing care. This is the care that most people do not want to talk about or even to think about. It's nursing care that is needed when you can't do for yourself. Nursing care is not cheap. A good facility will cost a minimum of $3,500 a month. That amount can gobble up savings and investments in no time.

I wouldn't worry about long-term care until you hit your fifties. The cost will vary among insurance companies, so make sure that the quotes you get represent the same type of benefits. Below are a few of the areas that you should look for:

- The *benefit period* should be no less than four years, preferably lifetime.
- The *elimination period* refers to how long you have to wait before benefits start. Ideally, day one is when you want it to commence; the wait period should not be greater than thirty days.
- The *daily benefit* amount refers to how much the policy will pay on a daily basis. A minimal amount is $100 for LTC in a facility, and $50 for your own home care.
- An *inflation rider* stipulates how much the coverage will increase annually.
- A *home health-care (HHC) clause* allows coverage provided by approved health-care providers in your home. HHC differs from LTC; long-term care individuals are not likely to be able to return to their home.

Before you sign on the dotted line, it's important to know what the policyholder will need to do to qualify for the benefits. These three components are usually the criteria:

- *Medical necessity* (i.e., your doctor says it's necessary care).
- *Activities of daily living (ADLs)*, which means that you are ambulatory; can bathe, dress, and feed yourself; can move about unattended; and are continent and able to use the toilet.
- *Cognitive impairment* refers to not being able to think or act clearly. The most common referrals will be for dementia and Alzheimer's disease.

The insurance company you select should not be new in the field of selling these policies. You want them to have been in the business of LTC for at least ten years; you should look for a company licensed in every state, not just yours. Companies such as CNA Insurance have done well for their policyholders. One source you can check out is AARP—American Association of Retired Persons. It makes sense that LTC is hot within this organization. The staff constantly monitor which insurance companies offer the best all-around products.

You want to know the ratings from the insurance raters—nothing below AA is acceptable. Since this is fairly new insurance, you will find more companies offering it, especially as the baby boomers move along the age wave. Ask the sales agents how often rates have been raised on existing policyholders. If rate increases have occurred more than a few times, stay away.

If I Were in Your Insurance Shoes

In 1905 a commission led by New York State Senator William Armstrong reported on the insurance industry:

The business is riddled with self-dealing, unsound investments, unsuitable policies, high pressure selling and unbridled sales expenses. Consumers take large losses when they drop expensive coverage that they shouldn't have bought and can't afford.

It is not much different today. Major insurance companies, such as Metropolitan Life, Equitable Life Insurance Society, and Crown Life were hit with massive lawsuits throughout the 1990s for misrepresentation, scams, and even selling phony retirement policies to nurses. Big moneys were paid in settlements.

> To protect yourself, you must be informed and take responsibility. Insurance moneys are very serious dollars.

If I were in your insurance shoes, here's what I would do:

- Use low-cost insurance. Work with a planner who recommends low-cost policies, not those that are bloated with commissions.
- Buy annual, renewable term insurance. In most of your key years for buying insurance, it will have the lowest cost.
- Get disability coverage.
- Stop smoking.
- Check out what Social Security will pay. Whenever I recheck my accumulated "earnings," I'm amazed at how much I'm supposed to get when I retire.

- Buy insurance from a Weiss-rated company and look for a company that has been rated "A+" for at least ten years. This would have saved thousands of policyholders the grief of losing money in the Executive Life fiasco.

- When the kids are gone and your financial responsibilities decline, you retire, or your spouse is self-sufficient, cancel your policy. And congratulate yourself.

Insurance—life, disability, health, and other forms—must be purchased with a Smart Money awareness. If not, you will overpay, buy the wrong type or buy at the wrong time, and not know it until years have passed.

This is not good. Having the right insurance coverage for your particular needs is imperative in building your financial security. This is one area where it makes sense to "hurry." The appropriate insurance sets a strong foundation in your home and your financial plan for your future. It's an absolute must in any financial plan.

WHEN THERE'S A WILL, THERE'S A WAY

Do not skip this section. One day a friend came over to my home. She admired a large, unframed painting of geraniums hanging in my breakfast area. She asked me whether, if I died before she did, I would leave it to her. "Absolutely," was my response. Knowing that I wasn't redoing my will in the immediate future—I immediately wrote a note and attached it to the back of the canvas. If I died, she got the painting. I then told my husband and daughters that I had put a note on it, and that if I died, they should give her the painting.

If you were to die tomorrow, does your family know what you want done with your assets, treasures, and, most importantly, if you have kids, with them?

> You will die someday. If it happens tomorrow, is your financial house in order or are you like the 75 percent of Americans who say tomorrow's another day?

Your daughters may love your jewelry. If you leave your jewelry to both of them, what happens if one moves 1,000 miles from the other? Who decides who gets what or how they share the jewelry?

Few people can reach perfect accord over what to do with mutually owned property. Anything that can't be divided should either be left to one person or be sold, and the proceeds split. When it comes to death and dying, few really plan for it or for those they leave behind. If no planning is done, those who are left behind may end up living with a monster.

I came across an article several years ago, saved it, and now pass on a portion of it to you. It has been repeated numerous times in Ann Landers's syndicated column. It was written by Judge Sam Harrod III (retired) of Eureka, Illinois. Since I first discovered it, I tracked Judge Harrod down—he's become one of my e-mail pals and has graciously given permission to include this portion of the article in this book.

IF YOU DON'T HAVE A WILL, YOUR STATE HAS ONE FOR YOU

The Statutory "Will" of John Doe

I, John Doe, make this my "will," by failing to have a will of my own choice prepared by my attorney.

1. I give one-half of all my property, both personal and real estate, to my CHILDREN, and the remaining one-half to my WIFE.
2. I appoint my WIFE as Guardian of my CHILDREN, if she survives me, but as a safeguard, I require that:
   a. my WIFE make written account every year to Probate Court, explaining how and why she spent money necessary for the proper care of our CHILDREN;
   b. my WIFE file a performance BOND, with sureties, to be approved by Probate Court, to guarantee she will properly handle our children's money;
   c. when our CHILDREN become adults, my WIFE must file a complete, itemized, written account of everything she has done with our children's money;
   d. when our SON and DAUGHTER become age 18, they can do whatever they please with their share of my estate;
   e. no one, including my WIFE, shall have the right to question how our CHILDREN spend their shares;

3. If my WIFE does not survive me, or dies while any of our CHIL-
   DREN are minors, I do not nominate a Guardian of our
   CHILDREN, but hope relatives and friends may mutually agree
   on one, and if they cannot agree, the Probate Court can appoint
   any Guardian it likes, including a stranger.
4. I do not appoint an Executor of my estate, and hope the Probate
   Court appoints someone I would approve.
5. If my WIFE remarries, the next husband
   a. shall receive one-third of my WIFE'S property;
   b. need not spend any of his share on our CHILDREN, even if
      they need support, and
   c. can give his share to anyone he chooses, without giving a
      penny to our CHILDREN.
6. I do not care whether there are ways to lower my death taxes, and
   know as much as possible will go to the Government, instead of
   my WIFE and our CHILDREN. In witness whereof I have completely failed to make a different will of my own choice with the
   advice of my attorney, because I really do not care to go to all that
   bother, and I adopt this, by default, as my "will."

(No signature required)

Sounds horrible, doesn't it? Without writing one, everyone does have a
will. The legal term is *intestate*—dying without a will. If you don't choose
one on your own, you get the one your state picks for you. Would you
choose this one that Judge Harrod has shared? Most likely, no.

> Wills should be left in writing. The only time an oral will is valid is
> when you are in imminent danger of death, there isn't much
> property involved, and several witnesses have heard you.

As your assets build up, you must begin to consider that you are mor-
tal. Rarely do I see people under age forty with a will that is properly put

together, and I do believe that wills should be written as soon as you begin to acquire any assets or *if you have children.*

The average working person spends more than 10,000 days making money. Take a couple of days out to inventory what you have and then start getting down on paper where you want it to go when you no longer are alive. Unfortunately, more than 75 percent of those who will die today won't have a written will. When you don't, your resident state will step in and assist your heirs in determining exactly where the assets will go. At that point there are no guarantees as to who will get what.

MAKE IT SO, AT LEAST TEMPORARILY

A will is critical in your financial plan, and it should be written now. If you don't have an attorney, at least sit down and write up what you want done in case of your death. This is called a *holographic will,* a will that is handwritten by you. In a holographic will you do the following:

- Record your name, permanent address (and, if applicable, secondary address), place of birth, and marital status.

- If you are married, have your spouse do the same. If there are any previous marriages, make sure that information is included, and include the names and addresses of your immediate family—children (birth, adoptive, and step-) and parents.

- Include the legal titles of any trusts or other instruments you have created that are in effect. If you are entitled to, or receive, any pensions, profit sharing, or investment distributions, include that information. All insurance policies should be identified with the name of the issuing company, the policy numbers and beneficiaries—both primary and secondary. If you have coverage through your employer under a group policy, be sure to state so.

- Compile a list of all your assets and present market values if you know them. If you own assets under a different name from your current one, make sure that both are specified.

- Identify where any safe deposit boxes are located.

- If you own stocks, bonds, limited partnerships, retirement accounts, passbooks, time deposits, IOUs payable to you, or any other marketable assets, identify what you have and, if at all possible, the dates you acquired them and the original cost. It's a good idea to specify the location of your previous tax returns for the last three years.

- You need to identify someone to manage your estate from the time of your death until the distribution of your assets. This person is known as the *executor* or *executrix* of your estate. Determine what your plans are for your beneficiaries; then state them.
- If you have kids, whom do you (and they) want to serve as a guardian if you die? If your beneficiaries will be under eighteen years of age, you will need to name a trustee to manage your assets until an actual distribution can be granted.
- Lastly, sign your holographic will.

This document acts *only as a temporary instrument.* I strongly recommend that you have an attorney who specializes in estate planning look it over and make whatever changes are necessary. An addendum, or codicil, can be added to your will when any changes are warranted.

> If you have a holographic will, you may question the need for an attorney. There are two good reasons to employ one. First, tax laws keep changing. If you aren't an expert in estate law, get a specialist's input. Second, an attorney can help ensure your will says *exactly* what you mean.

If you have a previously dated will, state in your new one that it revokes it. In addition, destroy any and all copies of your old will. If any of your assets are of sentimental value, do yourself a favor and attach to your will a letter of intent that states exactly who gets which belongings. If the majority of your property is divided by percentages, anything included in your letter of intent will be excluded from a percentage distribution of the primary estate. Why, you might wonder? Imagine you have a strand of pearls that your grandmother left you, and you know that your second of four daughters loves them. In a percentage distribution, she would get a quarter of the strand. Not very practical.

> For the do-it-yourselfers, one of the best guides is the *Simple Will Book* by Denis Clifford. It's available in many bookstores or you can contact Nolo Press at 950 Parker St., Berkeley, CA 94710.

Your holographic will may be quite clear to you but vague to others who read it. A trip to the local court may be necessary to determine what you really meant by "Susan Mary is to get my pearls"—is that niece Susan or daughter Susan? For a fairly simple will an attorney should charge from $150 to $300—but you can pay big dollars if you are complex. Execute only one will. For extras, make photocopies.

Anytime there is a new tax law, ask your attorney if it impacts you. To change a will you can (1) make a new one that revokes all wills and codicils before it or (2) tear it up. This is important. One of my clients, Laura, had originally created a holographic will. A few years later she created a new one. Unfortunately, she didn't destroy all the copies she had made of the first one. Laura died of breast cancer a few years after she had done the second holographic will, one that was substantially different from the first. Because the first had not been "called back," the court ended up saying that it stood and invalidated her second will.

If you choose route #2, do it in front of witnesses and state to them that the earlier will is no longer valid. Make sure you track down any copies and destroy those, too.

One last special scenario: If you have a disabled child, a will is critical. A disabled child (having little or no money) can usually qualify for some form of government aid. For advice on how to get help, one of the best resources is your state or local Association for Retarded Citizens. Ask for the names of lawyers experienced in your state's public-assistance laws. For the booklet *How to Provide for Their Future,* send $8 to the Association for Retarded Citizens, P.O. Box 1047, Arlington, TX 76004.

You probably feel that gathering up all this information and getting it down in writing is a pain in the neck. To be sure, it can be tedious and time-consuming. I'll guarantee you, though, that you won't regret doing it. Don't put it off. If you care for your spouse, children, parents, friends, and your community, this will become a priority. *Do it now.*

Summing Up—What's Next?

You are. You have the information to go forward. You know where you spend money and know what you are worth. Within a few weeks, you should have the right insurance and a will in place. You are maximizing your liquid moneys in money market funds. By now, you have contacted Social Security to determine what benefits you have earned, and you have looked up any other pension plan that you are covered under. And you know what professionals to consult with to shape the future nest egg you desire.

It's time for you to vocalize, if you haven't already, and visualize where you want to be in five, ten, fifteen, twenty . . . however many years it takes to get you into your eighties and nineties. You begin planning by dealing with many of the issues you have been reading about in this book. Your first step is to look at setting objectives. Your own. Then, begin to look at ways to invest your cash, enhance your income, and place your money in investments that will create growth (income, or both) and allow you to incorporate all your Smart Money Moves.

> There are two key ways to plan for your money to grow—save it and invest it. Do both; then watch what it will do!

---

10 Smart Money Moves in Creating and Implementing a Financial Plan

1. **Determine what your money resources are and where you spend your money.**

2. **If you work for pay and participate in a pension, profit sharing, or 401(k) plan, find out from your employer what the present value is and what the projected payout is for when you estimate you will retire.**

3. **If you aren't covered by any type of retirement plan at work, start an IRA now.** If you don't have all the moneys to fund the entire $2,000, set up a monthly plan to place up to $166 each month in the IRA of your choice.

4. **Find out how much life insurance you have.** Call one of the low-cost insurance companies identified in this chapter and get a quote on what a $100,000 and $300,000 policy would cost for someone your age.

5. **Make an inventory of all your assets.** You need this for the completion of a statement of your net worth.

6. **If you don't have a current will, begin the process of writing one, even if you intend on having an attorney prepare one for you.** Why?—it gets you started.

7. **Contact Social Security at 800-772-1213 and determine how much you will receive when you begin to withdraw funds.**

8. **Explore the cost of disability insurance.** Call at least three insurance brokers so that you have three independent quotes.

9. **Read *The Millionaire Next Door* by Thomas J. Stanley and William D. Danko (Pocket Books).** You will be amazed to learn that the person is more like you than the folks who drive a Rolls Royce. Your millionaire neighbors may be unknown to you by their appearance—they drive Fords, shop at Sears and JC Penney . . . they even clip store coupons!

10. **Be creative and find ways to trim bucks.** Look at the things that you do on a consistent basis that cost you money—such as when you pay someone for service. What if you didn't have a manicure every week? What if you washed your car every other week (or did it yourself)? What if you cut out eating out one meal a month (or a week)? What if you checked books out of the library instead of buying them, or traded them with a friend? What if you swapped used CDs and tape cassettes with friends? What if you colored your hair at home yourself instead of at the salon every six weeks? What if you shampooed your pets instead of taking them to the grooming shop? If you smoke, how much money is going up in smoke each week? How much money can you salt away by cutting out nonessentials?

The next Smart Money Move explores the concept of tithing—paying yourself.

Tithe to Yourself

4

Every woman needs a purse of her own. Women live longer than men do, and many are single more years than they are married. That means every woman needs to have the financial resources to support herself. Saving is the beginning. Investing comes later. For some, saving is an easy task; for others, incredibly difficult.

If you are a reader of the Bible, you probably remember that the concept of tithing is introduced in the book of Genesis. Throughout the Old and New Testaments, a 10 percent tithe to your faith is presented as an opportunity.

Tithing to yourself is also an opportunity. It's a faithful financial investment to and for you. Too many times, we let our age influence us—as in "I've got years to plan, to save, to invest. I'll start a program for my financial retirement (dream home, going back to school, taking a sabbatical) next year (or when I'm thirty, forty, fifty, whatever)." Money may be tight, so any idea of putting something aside is at the bottom of your To Do List.

My goal is to get you to *move paying yourself to the top of your money expense list*—to "pay yourself" (save what you spend) a minimum of 10 percent of your gross income, making it a monthly expense item just like your rent or mortgage payment each month.

> Tithing to yourself means that you promise to set aside a specific
> percentage of your income each month for you. It isn't for your

favorite charity or church. Nor for your vacation fund. Nor for gifts. It isn't for (fill in the blank). This *is* for your future safety net.

This money, your tithe, will seed your future nest egg. Yes, the one that will keep that roof over your head, the good food you love on your table, and the elimination of any possibility of being a bag lady. You may think, "I'm pushed to my limits. Paying myself first is impossible. Money goes for taxes, for food, for housing, for insurance; there's never enough. My money runs out before the end of the month, every month."

Does it? Let's look at what a lowly penny could do in a month.

BECOMING PENNY-WISE

How many times have you been around others who seem to have all the answers . . . to everything, sometimes even before you get the full question out? Here's a stumper to throw at them. Ask, "How many days will it take for you to become a millionaire if a penny doubles each day?" The answer: twenty-nine days. Beginning with one cent on the first day and doubling it, you would have two cents the second day, four cents the third day, and so on. On the twenty-eighth day you would have $1,342,177.28!

A Month of Pennies

1)	2)	3)	4)	5)	6)	7)
.01	.02	.04	.08	.16	.32	.64
8)	9)	10)	11)	12)	13)	14)
1.28	2.56	5.12	10.24	20.48	40.96	81.92
15)	16)	17)	18)	19)	20)	21)
163.84	327.68	655.36	1,310.72	2,621.44	5,242.88	10,485.76
22)	23)	24)	25)	26)	27)	28)
20,971.52	41,943.04	83,886.08	167,772.16	335,544.32	671,088.64	1,342,177.28

From one cent to $1,342,177.28

When you think of that amount, all beginning with a penny four weeks prior, the sum total is quite awesome. So, I throw out this question to you: "Are you ready to start making your millions . . . today?" It all starts with paying yourself.

It would be grand if you knew you would receive a tidy inheritance that would create money until you wanted or needed it. It would be great if your work paid you unbelievable amounts every day. Or if your spouse owned a money machine, and you would never again want for anything. Or if whatever you do generates unbelievable amounts of money.

You and I know that these scenarios are improbable. You could get an inheritance, of course, but one that is a bottomless money pit? Probably not. You may well be rewarded at your work, but will your annual pay exceed your wildest dreams? Hummmm . . . most likely not, at least when you work for someone else. What about Mr. Moneybags knocking on your door to say, "Be mine and you shall have unlimited access to all my assets"? Again, maybe, maybe not. And then there is your personal talent bank. Does everything you do or touch turn to gold? Do you have the Midas touch? How about your becoming the next Bill Gates? Maybe, maybe not.

The Month of Pennies example represents what a minor investment could do over a period of time. Yes, I know it's a stretch, but it opens a new door to your money thinking. It's a great wake-up call that illustrates what can happen with a consistent savings and investment plan—one that is put into play when you begin to loosen up and redirect money.

WHERE DOES YOUR MONEY GO?

In order to tithe and save, it's essential to know where your money goes. Do you? When I worked with clients, I often heard the statement "My money is gone before the end of the month." OK, I'll accept that simple statement. Here's my response—where does it go? "For essentials," you might respond. Really? If you are like most women I know and have worked with, there are a few kiss-off dollars flowing through your fingers, sometimes on a daily basis. "Kiss-off dollars? What are kiss-off dollars?" you ask.

They're the moneys that you spend for nonessentials, the "wants" of your life. Needs, on the other hand, are food, shelter, warmth, transportation, clothes, and such items. Needs can become wants when the Ford is traded for the BMW, the basic house for the mansion, the wool coat for the fur, the chicken for the filet mignon, the still-good outfit for a different colored one—do you get the picture I'm painting? Moneys that most likely won't come back to you (the exception could be in the house) and moneys that are spent on items that make you feel good are usually spent on wants. They are kiss-off dollars.

Lots of kiss-off dollars are spent in small dribbles—$3 for a magazine, $1 for a soda, $7 for lunch out, $8 for an evening movie ticket, money for late returns on rented videos, valet parking (instead of walking two blocks or using the street meters), drive-through eating, buying name-brand anything (versus the generic kind), buying a newspaper daily instead of having it delivered, buying when you need things (rather than planning to tap into sales), having your hair colored at a salon instead of doing it yourself, ditto with a manicure, smoking (a pack a day is over $1,400 a year!), shampooing your pooch at the doggie salon instead of in your shower, buying through most catalogues. Kiss-off moneys land in the sinkhole—gone, gone, gone, and never to be seen again.

So, you get to do that detailed exercise: track down where the bucks go, every nickel and dime. Do you write checks for everything? Or, do you like the feel of the green stuff, paying for everything from entertainment to eating out, from clothes to gasoline with cash? Do you try to charge everything on a credit card? Do you hit the ATM whenever you need cash, not using checks or credit cards?

Beginning today, you must become a sleuth. Every dollar, dime, and penny should be tracked for the next three months. The reason for a three-month period is to make sure you include any quarterly payments, such as car or home insurance.

Get a spiral pad or notebook and label the pages for different items—meals out (note which one it is), clothing, sundries, insurance, car and transportation expenses, groceries, entertainment, credit card and debt payments (not mortgage), household repairs and maintenance, mortgage or rent, gifts, health care, utilities, savings, taxes (don't forget to count the amounts withheld from paychecks), child care, child support, alimony, education, pets, and, of course, investments, retirement deposits, and other such expenses. Don't forget to include a category for unaccountable cash—it happens. As you do this, you will probably come up with a few categories of your own.

Smart Money Cash-Flow Statement

Alimony
_____

Car
_____

Child care
_____

Child support
_____

Clothing
_____

Credit card payments
_____

Debt & loan payments
_____

Education
_____

Entertainment
_____

Gifts
_____

Insurance
_____

Investments
_____

Health care
_____

Household repairs & maintenance
_____

Meals out
_____

Miscellaneous
_____

Miscellaneous
_____

Miscellaneous
_____

Miscellaneous
_____

Mortgage
_____

Other
_____

Other
_____

Other
_____

Other
_____

Other
_____

Pets
_____

Rent
_____

Retirement accounts
_____

Savings
_____

Taxes
_____

Transportation (other than car)
_____

Unaccountable cash
_____

Utilities
_____

Vacation & trips
_____

Total cash out

If you have a computer, invest in a personal finance software package, such as *Quicken* or *Microsoft Money.* The cost is approximately $50. Either will crunch numbers and simplify the tracking of your money. The only thing you have to do is enter in the correct amounts. At the end of each day, you input all your expenditures.

> I know—this activity can be a real pain in the neck. It takes time, something you may not feel that you have in abundance. But it is critical and needs to be done for three months. If you skip it, you will undermine your efforts to get control of your finances.

WHERE DOES YOUR MONEY COME FROM?

Now, let's flip the coin. In order to start saving and tithing to yourself, you have to know what all your monetary resources are. Your next step is to identify where your income comes from—it's a lot easier than probing where it goes. Do you ever think in the terms of *gross* income and *net* income? Your paycheck is a good example. Gross is what you start with before all the deductions are taken—federal and state taxes, Social Security (FICA), contributions to charitable causes such as United Way, health-care insurance, retirement accounts, loan payments, and savings payments.

You may even have more deductions than the ones listed above. The bottom line (net income) is what's left over. It's the amount you usually deposit into your checking account. This is the amount that you have for paying for all the other items that you need or want, under the category of living expenses. It is not unusual to ignore all the withholdings that normally occur. You may be surprised to find that you really don't know why certain amounts are being withheld or what percentage they represent of your monthly gross income.

> Don't ignore the small change—it all adds up, including the pennies.

Get your most recent paycheck stub. Most companies detail the amounts withheld and paid to taxing agencies, as well as other withholdings that you have authorized. These amounts usually reflect the current pay period as well as an accumulated total for the year.

Reading Your Paycheck Stub

Total Income from Salary
How much is withheld for all taxes?
How much is withheld for retirement purposes?
How much is deducted for other purposes?
Total Amount Withheld
Net Moneys Available (total salary minus total withheld)

The next step is to identify what your other sources of income are. Categories such as gifts, inheritances, trusts, investments, savings, money market funds, annuities, capital gains, dividends, interest, bonuses, retirement and pension accounts, rental property, refunds, and selling stuff you don't want or need all come to mind as other income sources.

Other Sources of Money

1 _____

2 _____

3 _____

4 _____

5 _____

6 _____

What's left over? Ideally, your income should exceed your expenses. If it is equal, or if your expenses exceed your income, it is time to ask yourself before you buy anything more as a consumer, "Do I *really need* this . . . or do I *want* it?" If it is a *want,* don't buy it. Period. There is no way you will be able to start saving money until you achieve leftover funds.

DISAPPEARING CASH

One of the biggest culprits of cash misuse is your local ATM. In fact, ATMs lead the list for cash abuse. If your money runs out before the end of the month, this is the first place to sleuth for that disappearing cash. It's common to forget to enter withdrawals in your check register, to withdraw more cash than you originally intended to, or to return to the ATM to get more. Where does it all go? Five dollars here, two dollars there, and all of a sudden, there's no more.

Major recipients of your loose cash include entertainment, meals out, and convenience foods. If you are truly serious about saving money, here is where you start. Dump the ATM card; then significantly reduce expenditures for entertainment, meals out, and convenience food. Identify the items you have purchased that were really *wants* and not *needs.* You'll save hundreds of dollars every month—dollars you will redirect to your Tithe Fund, your new cash haven.

CREATING YOUR LIQUIDITY FUND

At this point, you're probably reading this section because it follows what you have just read. Perhaps you're reading it after a time-out of the last three months spent in tracking your moneys. Either way, you have identified or started the process of discovering where your money comes from and where it goes.

I'm going to assume that you have been successful in reducing your outflow and have actually started to save money. With a new purse of your own, it's time to create and build your *liquidity fund*—a three-to-six-month stash of money you can access within a few days. Remember my client with the over-stuffed green chair? That chair held her liquidity fund! Your fund should at least be earning interest as it sits waiting for your emergency command.

Once you have determined what your monthly income is and necessary expenses are, one more step is needed. Assume that you (your spouse or both of you) are working for pay, something happens, and you are off work for several months. During this time, you won't receive your salary of $3,500 a month. While you don't get your salary, taxes will no longer be withheld, you won't contribute to your 401(k) retirement account, and you could suspend any contributions you usually make until you are back on your feet.

Those amounts ($980, $175, and $20) would be tallied ($1,175) and deducted from your gross salary of $3,500, leaving you $2,325, one month's needed income. That number could be further reduced if you didn't spend all of the $2,325, if you further reduced expenditures (e.g., your transportation costs of driving back and forth to work) or received any type of disability insurance payment.

Figuring Your Liquidity Fund Needs	
Total income from salary sources	$3,500.00
How much is withheld for all taxes? (federal, state, FICA)	**980.00**
How much is withheld for retirement purposes? (5 percent of $3,500)	**175.00**
How much is deducted for other purposes? (United Way)	**20.00**
Total amount withheld	**$1,175.00**
Net moneys available (total salary minus total withheld)	**$2,325.00**
Liquidity Fund (minimal = three months × $2,325)	**$6,975.00**

The new figure of $2,325 represents what you really need in income each month if a "worse case" scenario occurs. That amount, multiplied by three to six, is the amount you want to accumulate before you start investing. It comprises your ideal liquidity fund.

WHERE TO STASH CASH

Your new savings should earn the most amount of interest that is safely possible. Your choices for where to stash your cash include a money market fund (the type you can get from a mutual fund company, a full-service brokerage firm, or a discount one), your credit union, savings and loan association, or a bank. My personal choice would be with a mutual fund company or brokerage firms. Why? Money market funds with the mutual fund companies usually pay a higher rate, anywhere from one-half to one-and-one-half percent above the other safe and liquid possibilities. It's another way to add to your savings. All of the money market funds will pay more than the average passbook-savings rate. There are thousands of mutual funds. Every "family" of funds (e.g., Janus, Fidelity, Vanguard) has a money market fund.

A money market fund allows you to write checks and withdraw your funds whenever you want, without penalty. Money market funds definitely meet the definition of an ideal holder of liquidity-fund moneys. When first introduced on Wall Street in the 1970s, the public didn't jump to put its cash in. Today, these funds are as common as checking accounts.

When purchasing and investing in a money market fund, you should do the following:

- Determine the current interest rate and compare it with those of other funds (you will find a weekly listing in the *Wall Street Journal,* available at your local library) or check financial information on the Internet.
- Make sure that you have check-writing privileges.
- Ask if there is a service fee or a charge for checks (most funds allow some checks to be cashed with no charge).
- Determine what minimum amount you need to invest to open and maintain the account. If your balance drops below the minimum, is there a fee?
- Determine if there is an annual fee (there shouldn't be).
- Ask if you get a monthly statement (you should) and your canceled checks back (most don't send them back).
- Ask what other services are available. Some money market funds offer a debit card, which works the same way a debit card would at your regular bank. Make sure to ask if there are any additional fees to use the debit card.
- Ask how interest is paid (the answer should be "daily").

Where do you find a good money market fund?

- The business section of your newspaper usually carries ads and you can call a company's 800 number for information and a prospectus to open an account.
- Your local brokerage can supply you with information.
- You can ask your friends what funds they use.
- If you already invest in mutual funds, contact their customer service; most fund families have money market funds in addition to their other funds.

- You can call a discount brokerage, such as Charles Schwab, which has its Schwab One Account with a minimal start-up of $5,000. As long as you maintain that minimum, annual fees are waived.
- Get a copy of *The Complete Money Market Guide* by William Donoghue. Everything you might need to know about money market funds can be found in this book, available in paperback. Donoghue is recognized as the father of the money market fund. His book remains the single best one on the market.
- Go on-line and tap into the Internet. Most likely, your local server will have a link that you can readily use to get into personal finance sites.

TREASURY SECURITIES

U.S. Treasury securities (bonds, notes, and bills) used to be the place that people with lots of money would stash some of their cash. Treasury bills ("T-bills") used to have a minimum buy in of $10,000. No more. In August 1998, the policy was changed so that treasury bills could be purchased with a minimum investment of $1,000. They have the shortest term (you buy them for three months, six months, or twelve months) and the least fluctuation in price in relation to interest rates. Treasury bills are purchased at discount. This means that if you want a $1,000 bill and the stated interest is 5 percent, you will actually pay $950 for a twelve-month bill. At the end of the twelve months, you will receive $1,000 back.

Treasury notes ("T-notes") have a minimum buy in of $1,000 with increments of $1,000. Their life ranges from two to ten years and they pay interest twice a year. Treasury bonds ("T-bonds") are the longest term, with a thirty-year period being the only offering. They pay interest twice a year, and have a minimum buy in of $1,000.

All interest is reported in the year it is received or, in the case of treasury bills, when the bill matures. If you bought a six-month T-bill in November, you wouldn't have to report the interest on your tax return until the following year. Interest is taxable on your federal income tax return, and is tax free on your state income tax return.

Treasury securities can be purchased from your bank, savings and loan, stockbroker, or financial planner; you can even go to the Federal Reserve Bank that serves your area. Some financial institutions will charge you for any purchases, so make sure you ask. The Federal Reserve does not add these charges.

Other Ways to Create a Tithe

Are there versions of paying yourself first? Sure, it doesn't have to be that you literally put 10 percent aside after you get paid. It can happen before and it can happen the way you pay a bill—like your mortgage.

Let Your Employer Partner with You

If you work outside your home for pay, a simple way to tithe to yourself is to participate in an automatic savings program through your employer, a bank, or a money market fund within a mutual fund. You can set up a withdrawal from your salary on a specific date or pay period. Your pay stub will show the withdrawal and payment. My experience is that if you don't get your hands on it, you don't spend it!

If you have a 401(k) or any other deferred type of program available through your employer, take advantage of it. These programs save tax dollars, and many employers will contribute moneys on your behalf. When this happens, think of it as a gift. If you contribute 6 percent of your salary to a plan and your employer matches it, that's quite a bonus, and it adds to your tithe to you.

To Roth . . . or Not to Roth

A new retirement animal has surfaced as the millennium rears its head. The Roth IRA offers some changes from the traditional IRA. With a traditional IRA you:

- May take a $2,000 deduction from your taxable income.
- Will be taxed on anything it earns via growth, dividends, or interest when you withdraw moneys at a later date. Under most circumstances, if you withdraw money before you are fifty-nine and a half, you are penalized 10 percent of the amount withdrawn and taxed at your income tax rate—Uncle Sam gets a big share.
- Must start withdrawing funds by the time you are seventy and a half.

With a Roth IRA you:

- May not take a deduction from your taxable income.
- Will not be taxed on any future earnings if you wait until you are fifty-nine and a half before you begin withdrawing your money.

Uncle Sam gets none of the accumulated growth during the time you have it. If you withdraw money before fifty-nine and a half, you will probably be hit with the 10 percent penalty on what you withdraw.
- Can defer withdrawing moneys to any age you wish.

If you are under fifty-five and have a traditional IRA, it may make tax and money sense for you to convert to a Roth IRA. You will be taxed on the increased value, but once these taxes are paid, everything becomes tax free, including any moneys you add to it. In 1998, Congress changed the law to allow those converting to spread the tax consequences over a four-year period. It might also make sense to leave your traditional IRA intact and start a new Roth IRA. If converting is a possibility, get input from a financial planner or accountant *before* you do anything involving a change.

Here's the bottom line: do everything you can to participate in the retirement-related plans available to you. If your employer offers one, sign up as soon as you can. Determine how much your employer will contribute in addition to what you put in; then maximize your contribution so you get as much as you can from both your employer and your paycheck. Make sure you consult with a financial planner or your accountant to adjust your withholding on your paycheck.

STOCKING UP WITH YOUR CHECKING AND SAVINGS ACCOUNT

On the twentieth of every month or the next closest business day, I know that several hundred dollars will be withdrawn from my personal checking account. Who takes it? One of the mutual funds that I have selected to invest in on a regular basis. Granted, initially I might forget a few times to enter the withdrawal on the check register. My husband first said, "Are you sure we can do this?" We did, and we both think this is a great way to salt away money and let it grow. Our only regret is that we hadn't started this process when we first learned that there was something called investing! Now, it's a regular habit, and those few hundred have grown to many thousands since I started the practice a few years ago.

You too can set up a regular investment program that directs moneys to stocks, mutual funds, and money market funds. All you need to do is contact the customer service representative with the financial institution you want to work and invest with, complete the necessary paperwork, and you are on your way.

Uncle Sam and Income Tax Refunds

One of my button pushers is the subject of tax refunds. When former clients, participants in my money workshops, family members, and friends tell me that they "love" getting the big refund check from their taxes every April, I cringe. Why do they do it? For that matter, if you get a refund, why do you do it? The answer is usually because you don't know any better or you think it's the only way to create an instant stash.

You may be wondering "How does this tie into saving and tithing?" Stretch with me just a bit. Aren't you trying to identify sources where money is misspent or frittered away? Getting a refund, any tax refund, is kissing off the use of your own money. Couldn't you have been earning interest on it? Investing it? Paying off any other debt you might currently have, including credit card balances? The answer to all these is yes.

The average refund for federal tax returns filed in 1998 was more than $1,000 per return. If you used those moneys on an ongoing basis to reduce credit card debt, you could have saved $180 to $200 in interest charges from the credit card company. If you did nothing but put the money in a passbook savings account, you would have been ahead at least $30 to $40. Or if you had the cash, and an incredible sale popped up for an item you needed, you would again have been way ahead because you could have bought it at a discount, for cash.

> Please, please think again. When you get a tax refund, you are making an interest-free loan to Uncle Sam—and he doesn't even send you a thank-you note.

Twice a year, you should take a close look at what your gross income is, how much tax has been withheld or paid in, and what kind of deductions you anticipate will occur. A good time to do this checking is in the first quarter, around tax-filing time, and within the fall months to see if you are on target for tax-withholding requirements. If you feel totally lost in the woods, a certified financial planner or your accountant should be able to unravel any mysteries fairly quickly. You need to ask these questions:

- Has anything different happened this year from last (or will it happen next year)? Such an occurrence would be the purchase of a home that creates tax-deductible interest greater (or less) than the amount you used to claim or, if you rented, than when there was no deduction allowed.

- What will my gross income be for the year? Determine if there are any additions or reductions from what was reported the previous year.
- Did I sell anything that would create a gain or a loss to be claimed on my return?
- Will I incur any additional taxes, such as real estate, that will be deductible this year and that I didn't have last year?
- Have I (or will I) make any contributions to charitable causes that will reduce my taxable income?
- What will my tax obligation be? It's amazing how accurate you can be with a W-4 (the employee withholding form that you fill out when you are first employed), a current tax table, and calculator. If what you are presently paying in is right on target for what you will owe overall, you are in good shape. But, if your calculations indicate that you have already paid in more than you need to, or that you may be short, action is called for. Your W-4 needs to be either increased or reduced in your total allowance declarations.

If you show an overpayment, an increase in the present number of allowances you declare will adjust the withholding amount and actually pay you more per paycheck. If you show a shortfall, you need to decrease the number of allowances you are declaring. Any refund simply means that you paid *too much* in taxes. Most likely, you wouldn't be willing to pay too much for items you normally purchase; taxes should be no different.

What do you do with the newfound money now coming in with your paycheck instead of as a one-time refund? You use it to reduce outstanding credit card balances, save it, or invest it. You can save it in a money market fund or you can invest it for *long-term growth,* not in an instrument that you think you will have to tap into within a few months.

A final warning—if it is appropriate for you to change your withholding allowances, especially to increase them to more than eight, your payroll department clerk may tell you that you can't. Do it anyway; the clerk is wrong. It may make sense to attach a simple statement that says, "I changed my withholding allowances because I purchased a home this year that now creates $10,000 more annually in tax deductions." An IRS agent would see that and immediately understand what is going on. Getting any future tax refunds is now a money taboo for you, since you understand that you can alter what is withheld.

The Year of the Child

In 1999, Congress declared the "Year of the Child" for parents. If you have kids, including college-age ones, money may be coming your way.

Take Credit for Your Kids

Most families will be able to claim the new $500 credit for each dependent child under the age of seventeen in 1999. This credit started in 1998 at the $400 level—if you missed out and you have kids, it would be a Smart Money Move to amend your 1998 return. Credits are terrific—they allow you to deduct directly from the overall amount you owe Uncle Sam. This is different from a deduction, which merely reduces the amount of taxable income.

To take advantage of this credit, you must meet the means test. For married couples filing jointly, your adjusted gross income must be $110,000 or less; for singles, the amount is $75,000. Your credit will be reduced by $50 for every $1,000 you have in income above the adjusted gross income thresholds. The credit is unique. It includes natural, adopted, foster, step-, and grandchildren, as long as they qualify as dependents.

If you owe no federal income tax at all for the year, you won't get any money back from the credit unless you have three or more qualifying children.

Tax Credits for Students

Two new credits have also been created for students of any age. The Hope tax credit is designated for students in their first or second year of college or postsecondary school. The student must be in school at least half-time and be participating in a degree or certificate program. You may claim up to $1,500 per student. Tuition and fees are included in the offset expense; books, and room and board are not.

The other credit is the Lifetime Learning credit. This credit does not have the half-time student requirement. It can be used for a one-time course to improve your skills. The maximum credit is $1,000 per year; this is a cumulative credit, meaning that that amount is the maximum that your household will be able to declare, even if you have five students. It's determined by taking 20 percent of the first $5,000 paid in fees and tuition, up to the maximum amount.

You may not take both credits in the same year for a single student. Married couples filing jointly get full credit for either program on adjusted gross incomes of up to $80,000. At $100,000, the credit is no longer available. Singles get it at up to $40,000, with a phase out at $50,000.

Deductions for Loan Interest

If you have student loans (as a student or parent), you can get a deduction or a write-off during the first sixty months of the loan repayment. You can take the deduction even if you don't file an itemized tax return. As with most IRS quasiperks, this deduction also has an income limitation. For married couples filing jointly, it's $60,000, phasing out at $75,000; for singles it's $40,000, phasing out at $55,000.

CREDIT CARD ROBBERS

I'm not talking about someone stealing your wallet or purse or somehow accessing your credit card numbers. I'm talking about the credit card folks who issue the cards. Right now, do you have any credit cards with balances? If you do, and if the interest being charged is in the double digits, call the 800 number listed on the back of the card. Say something such as this to a live voice:

> *I'm getting credit card offers daily to transfer my balance from your card to another at a substantially lower rate. Before I decide to fill in the application, transfer the balance, and terminate my account with you, will you reduce my interest rate? How much lower will you go?*

I don't care if you haven't recently received any offers in the mail; just go ahead and say you did. The lowest rate I've seen is 3.9 percent for the first six months. Ninety percent of the time, that phone representative has the authority to immediately reduce your rate by phone. (The Discover card is one that won't.) Take the person's offer, and then decide if it makes Smart Money Sense to apply for the new card anyway. If you do, after transferring the balance, cancel the old card.

Another way you get hit is by a high annual fee—the most common is $25. Again, use the same approach: "I'm being offered an account with no annual fee. Will you match it?"

In 1998 credit card companies began to aggressively raise their interest rates on outstanding balances for existing cardholders. They also introduced a high ($20 to $25 a pop) monthly charge if a customer went over his or her limit or was late on a payment. Even someone who pays off her balance in full each month could get hit with a late fee, if the payment came in late.

The reduction in credit card balances means you are saving an interest rate that can exceed 20 percent. A balance of $1,000 means that you could easily be paying $200 extra every year in credit card interest. Instead of paying the card company, pay yourself. As Martha Stewart says, it's a good thing.

MORTGAGE ESCROW ACCOUNTS
AREN'T WHAT THEY SEEM

If you are a first-time home buyer and don't have impeccable credit or a large down payment, you can be penalized. The mortgage company may require you to include your real estate taxes and home owner's insurance payments within your monthly mortgage payment.

If you can swing it, meaning that you will discipline yourself to set the money aside for your tax and insurance payments, don't include these extra payments with your mortgage. The lender ends up sitting with megathousands, even millions of dollars from many borrowers like you, and *never* pays you (or the other borrowers) one cent of interest. Such a deal! Instead, pay your insurance and real estate taxes when they are due. Remember the month of pennies? Every interest and investment dollar counts.

MORTGAGE SAVINGS FOR THE TAKING

One of the great things home owners can do is to pay extra on their mortgage account each year. Some financial advisors suggest adding to the monthly payment, others suggest sending in one extra payment during the year. Some will also advise you to get a fifteen-year, instead of the traditional thirty-year, loan.

It all depends. Check out the rates. Many of the mortgages available in the market today carry the same interest rate for both types. You need to do some shopping and check out your options. If they are the same, I would go with a thirty-year loan, knowing that I'm going to pay extra each year to reduce the life of the mortgage.

So what does that mean in dollars? Let's say you have a thirty-year loan. By making one extra payment a year, you will reduce the life of the loan to twenty-two years! A mortgage that you are paying $1,200 a month for means that you would pay a total of $432,000 over the thirty years. By accelerating it with an extra $1,200 each year, your total output comes to $316,800, a reduction of $115,200 from the amount you would have paid over the thirty years. Putting $115,200 in your nest-egg kitty sounds better than giving it to a mortgage company, right?

As a home owner, it's a Smart Money Move to truly determine the cost of financing your home. Home mortgages range anywhere from ten to forty years. Today, the most likely one you will choose is a fifteen- or thirty-year loan. One of the perks to getting a fifteen-year loan is that the interest rate may be lower than the more traditional thirty-year loan. On the other hand, because the loan is paid off in half the time, the payments are bigger. Let's take a look at $125,000 fifteen- and thirty-year loans.

	Thirty-year mortgage	*Fifteen-year mortgage*
Mortgage amount	$125,000	$125,000
Interest rate	7%	6 ½%
Monthly payment	$830	$1,083
Total payments	$298,800	$194,940

On a monthly basis, you will pay $253 more each month with the fifteen-year mortgage. But (and this is a **big** but), if you elected to go with the fifteen-year mortgage, the amount you would save is $103,860!

Here's what I do—I add 10 percent extra each month to my regular mortgage payment with a note to apply the additional amount toward reducing the principal of the loan. If I had a thirty-year loan, I would shop around for a fifteen-year one and then refinance. One thing to consider is that the extra payments you make will reduce the amount that you can claim as an interest deduction on your tax return at year-end. Let your accountant know so that it can be taken into consideration for future tax planning.

> One of your personal goals should be to have your home mortgage free when you retire. Accelerating your mortgage payments is the single best way to get it done (assuming that you don't have a windfall coming your way that could do it).

SUMMING UP—IT'S A GOOD THING

Tithing and paying yourself is a commonsense approach to seeding and growing your money future. Unfortunately, it is rarely put into practice. If your true goal is to be financially self-reliant, then tithing to yourself should become part of your monthly mantra.

> Expand the accepted definition of a tithe—the one that says write
> the 10 percent check each month. You can be creative. To me, it
> doesn't matter if your income is $1,000 or $10,000 a month—$100
> or $1,000 socked away every month builds incredible foundations.

With your new program of paying extra dollars to mortgages, eliminating refunds in your tax-filing future, using credit cards wisely, investing through your checking account, not paying unnecessary amounts to any creditor, and being a discriminating spender ("Do I really need this?"), don't be surprised to find that you will exceed that 10 percent goal! Definitely, a Smart Money Move.

---

10 SMART MONEY MOVES
TO TITHE TO YOURSELF

1. Stop overpaying your taxes and getting refunds.

2. Don't charge anything unless it is essential.

3. Pay off your credit card balances.

4. Always ask, "Do I need this or do I just want it?"

5. Avoid using your ATM card.

6. Reduce the times you eat out by 50 percent.

7. Buy only needed stuff (food excluded) when it is on sale.

8. Commit to a regular investment program, funded like your housing costs—on a monthly basis.

9. Don't buy disposable items—they cost more.

10. Reduce the use of convenience items, including food—they also cost more.

Create a Fantastic, Smart Money Team

5

In the world of money management, it is almost impossible to think you "know it all." The money game can be complex. Even after you have set specific financial goals for yourself, you need a definite strategy. Haphazard investing won't do.

This chapter is not intended simply to encourage you to seek advice from "wise" men and women, but to help you also identify those specialists and experts who can help you evolve and implement a coherent, consistent financial plan, one that is appropriate for you. Certainly you can find a lot of information on your own, but there is a certain wisdom in experience—experience that the professionals already have.

There are a myriad of reliable publications, such as the *Wall Street Journal, Forbes, Barron's, Business Week, Fortune, Newsweek, Time, U.S. News & World Report, Worth,* and *Money* magazines; *Value Line Investment Survey*; and a variety of tax advisory newsletters you can subscribe to. There are even some good TV stations and programs that deal intelligently with money matters. CNN, CNNfn, CNBC, and MSNBC air numerous money and business programs every day. These shows routinely refer you to their on-line addresses to get additional information.

The Internet has become one of the hottest and most active resources for financial information. *Money* magazine birthed *money.com*, an Internet money magazine, in the fall of 1998. It literally hooks you into just about any money-related Internet address you might need. AOL, the most popular of on-line systems, routinely has money-related items on their "You've got mail" announcement that connects subscribers with its personal finance link—*AOL.personalfinance.com*. Your computer and phone line are a keyboard away from zillions of financial information. All you need do is type in a keyword or two—*mortgages, refinance, stocks, mutual funds, annuities, financial planners, credit cards.* You think of it; there's information across those wires!

But you can overdo it, ending up with information overload. How? You inundate and bury yourself with too much data, so that you end up having no time left for strategizing, managing what you have, and investing. Remember the phrase—one for the money, two for the show, three to get ready, and four to go? A common problem becomes that overload gets you stuck on three—it's hard to go!

> "Be willing to take a little help" is probably, in general, good advice. But before looking for some experts, keep this in mind: whomever you deal with should have been in his or her field of expertise for at least five years—let them make their beginner mistakes with someone else.

A word of caution is in order here. People who advise you about your money may also receive a commission for investment products that you buy through them. Do not hesitate to ask if there is a commission to be paid on what you are being offered and how much it is. If you choose to go ahead and place your money, you at least know who gets what. I call that being informed.

> The key is to utilize the best informational sources available so you can analyze the trends of the past and the present to maximize the future of your investments.

As you explore the variety of sources today—whether newspapers, magazines, TV, radio, the Internet, or your friends, you may find yourself inundated with information and confused by all the variety of "experts" who have just the right theory for a particular moment. What you want is someone who is available, consistent, and reasonably experienced. What's that mean?

- Available means that your phone calls will be returned and any questions you have will be responded to within a reasonable period of time—usually within twenty-four hours.
- Consistency refers to always keeping your objectives under consideration when recommending any type of strategy or investment for you. An inconsistent advisor could make suggestions simply to get a commission, even if it isn't the right fit for your objectives.
- Experience refers to the simple fact that life is a little more complex today. So are money issues and decisions. An experienced advisor will openly consult with or refer you to another expert if your situation demands it.

It will not be unusual to get differences of opinions and advice from the advisors you consult with. Some recommendations may be totally valid at the time they are given but turn out to be wrong as time progresses. You may have legal recourse when you act on bad advice. The problem is that it is very difficult and costly to confirm that the advice you were given was inappropriate or due to negligence. Any kind of litigation costs a substantial amount, and I'm convinced that in most cases the only person who wins is the attorney.

To help avoid such a pitfall, therefore, I recommend that when you sit down with your "experts" obtain the following in *writing*:

- What a particular investment is all about
- What the financial projections are in both the best and worst cases
- Who the principals are who will be managing and making decisions
- What the risks are

I emphasize once again, don't work with anyone who hasn't been in the field of expertise for at least five years. With these bits of cautionary advice in mind, who are the experts and what should you expect from them?

WHO ARE THEY? WHOM DO YOU USE?

Throughout your money life, you will use a variety of individuals to advise you. Bankers, financial planners, stockbrokers, attorneys, insurance agents, and real estate agents are a few of the most common consultants.

Bankers

The first money professional most of us work with is usually at our local bank. You probably didn't really think that bank personnel were members of your team. Most people merely make deposits through the car depository window or borrow money for the purchase of a car, and that's it. Your banker can do a lot; however, you need to know how to fully use a bank's services.

Banks, and the services they offer, have changed substantially over the past ten years. Banks have always been a mainstay in any community. Today nothing would make a banker happier than having all of your financial business—from your deposits to mortgages, insurance, loans, investments, and trusts. The person who is your primary contact at the bank should not be a junior member of its management team. You want someone who knows you and is willing to work with you through the bad times, not just the good ones.

Bankers are often flexible and able to work with you over the phone. Last year I had a new home built. The only problem was that the one I was living in had not sold when it was time to close escrow on the new one—which meant that I didn't have all the money needed for the down payment. With one phone call, however, I had the money commitment from the banker. I was able to do that only because I had developed a solid relationship before I needed the money. You want to do the same.

> Do yourself a tremendous favor and go introduce yourself in person to the manager of your bank. You will be remembered.

When you are considering putting money in the bank, ask the banker exactly how much you will earn on your funds—the bottom line. For example, don't accept a statement that says 4 percent. You want to know 4 percent of what, and paid how often—is it simple interest, a daily average rate, a current rate, or an annual rate?

The bottom-line question is that if you deposit money today, what will be the earned amount of interest six months from now? That way you can compare apples with apples to determine where you want to deposit your money.

Certified Financial Planners

Because of the confusing inundation of information you're likely to encounter, the variety of theories, which often conflict with one another (they are rooted in the individual's outlook or expertise, after all), and the complexities of today's financial arena, you should start out seeking an experienced financial planner.

The designation of CFP was created in the 1970s, and it is granted by the College of Financial Planning in Denver, Colorado. CFPs have taken multiple courses over a period of time in a variety of financial areas, and they must take continuing education courses to retain the CFP designation.

A CFP can project your net worth and earnings in future years based on financial data that you provide. Evaluations and recommendations on investments, insurance, and tax planning are a normal range of a CFP's services. Check out how they are compensated. Some charge a flat fee to develop a financial plan, others charge on an hourly basis, some will receive commissions on products and investments they sell to you, and others do a combination of all three.

> Your planner should be a qualified professional who will act like a contractor or general engineer to help you devise a game plan and locate or orchestrate subcontractors (other financial professionals) who are experts in specific fields of investing.

The financial planner is similar to a family practice doctor—she keeps track of you overall, and, when necessary, may refer you to other financial or legal specialists. Your planner's primary function is to create a plan that fits with your objectives and needs and then to create the strategy to implement it.

Most financial planners have a variety of licenses. All licenses require training and testing in a specific field before they are granted. Your planner will be *able* to sell a variety of financially oriented investment products. This does not mean that she must sell these. Some planners work with clients only on a fee basis (i.e., per hour), a percentage of the assets that are managed, or a set amount per plan. Other planners make recommendations. If you decide you want to invest, there may be a commission paid to the planner for it.

The majority of financial institutions—banks, insurance companies, or stock brokerage and accounting firms—offer some form of personal financial management. It's important to ask what type of clients they work with—some have minimal requirements for net worth, others are glad to see anyone who is ready to work on their financial lives.

Finding a planner will take some work on your part. If you are new to your area, don't know any financial professionals, or have not received

referrals from friends or colleagues, contact the International Association
of Financial Planners (IAFP) Registry or the Institute of Certified Financial
Planners (ICFP) for a referral in your area:

> IAFP Registry
> Two Concourse Parkway, Suite 800
> Atlanta, GA 30328
> 404-395-1605
>
> Institute of Certified Financial Planners
> 760 E. Eastman, Suite 301
> Denver, Colorado 80231
> 800-282-7526

The IAFP membership comprises accountants, bankers, real estate agents
and brokers, securities representatives, money managers, financial consultants, attorneys, and insurance agents and brokers—just about anyone
who works in the money field. Presently, the IAFP has some 100,000 members. A directory is available that lists its members. You'll find the association in the Yellow Pages under Financial Planners.

The ICFP has a different membership base. It comprises only those who
have completed the two-year course sponsored by the institute that is
headquartered in Colorado. Someone's having a CFP degree doesn't guarantee that his or her advice will be the right fit for you. Having the degree
means that the individual has gone the extra miles to learn more about
financially related fields and concepts than, let's say, a stockbroker or insurance agent (most CFPs also have both those licenses).

When selecting a financial planner, the chemistry you feel with that person is important. If someone makes you uncomfortable, take a pass. Your
planner should respect you as an individual and a woman—remember what
both men and women said in the Oppenheimer survey, that women did
not receive the level of respect men did.

If possible, get recommendations from friends and acquaintances and
ask specific questions that relate to your circumstances, not the friend's who
referred you. Most people love to talk about how great things are—ask your
referral sources who they have dealt with that they *haven't liked* or cared for.
Ask why. Whomever you go with should be available, return phone calls
within twenty-four hours, and explain—until you fully understand—what
and why something is being recommended. Your planner must be consistent—she shouldn't whipsaw you with multiple suggestions every time you
ask for advice. As with any professional you work with in the financial

arena, experience is mandatory. Your advisor should have at least five years' experience.

Know how your financial planner is compensated. Preferably, she shouldn't earn her living solely from commissions. A fixed fee (usually an hourly rate) for consultation enables your planner to give you an unbiased evaluation of the financial options that fit your objectives.

Financial planning is a fairly young industry. It has grown tremendously since the early 1980s. In fact, professionals with a major West Coast research firm who did a study on financial planning were so impressed with the growth potential that they terminated the relationship with their company and opened up their own financial planning firm in Northern California!

Advisors and planners crop up overnight—and, like mushrooms, not all of them are "edible." Frances Lear, publisher of the defunct *Lear's* magazine, went into the advisory business for a short time after she closed down *Lear's*. She produced a videotape, *Take Control of Your Life*, all about money. Her advisor-guru in the tape is Harry Browne, a long-time proponent of gold. Except for a few good "up" years, his advice has been mediocre for the most part. Take a pass.

Just about anyone can become an "expert" in the public's eye—yet the person's qualifications and performance might be graded "D" or "F." My advice is to avoid the Lears and the Brownes of the world by reviewing their report cards.

> One additional caution—if a divorce is in the works, any financial planner you and your spouse used as a couple should remain aboveboard with you both. No sides can be taken, and you both must be given the same information at the same time. If one spouse receives information that favors him or her, the other spouse could file a lawsuit against the planner. The couple's original financial planner should maintain as neutral a position as possible.

STOCKBROKERS

If you are contemplating the purchase of stocks or bonds, you will work with someone who is a stockbroker or, at least, who has a license to act as one. The securities industry has changed a lot over the last decade. Stockbrokers now buy and sell just about anything you could imagine relating to money—stocks, bonds, mutual funds, limited partnerships, options, money market funds, U.S. treasuries, insurance, annuities, and mortgages to name just a sample of what they can deal with.

Some brokers specialize in specific industries. One of my friends is recognized as a top expert in a technology-related area. Another invests exclusively in the commodities area. When I was a broker and had clients who were interested in technology-related companies, I referred them directly to my friend. If clients called about pork bellies and wheat, they were passed on to an associate very quickly. Although I could buy and sell commodities at that time, I was basically clueless as to how they "really" worked. Jonathon wasn't and did fairly well for his elite clientele.

Some brokerage firms or "houses" pressure their brokers to sell their products to the exclusion of others. Thus, some brokers merely parrot what their particular parent firm outlines in investment recommendations. For a strictly unbiased approach, you must keep your eyes focused on what is going on in the supply and demand area and make decisions about stock purchases on your own.

During the 1990s, several industries have shined—electronics, comput-ers, technology, and health care, and personal grooming products pop into mind as I write this. Feet have also been hot—the folks who make Nike and Reebok shoes. Gillette shaved their competition when the Lady Sensor razor was introduced for women and the new Mach III for men. Pfizer hit gold when Viagra debuted in 1998.

> Stockbrokers get paid by commission, so if you are demanding a substantial amount of their time and producing few results in the form of income, they may soon lose interest in you.

If you feel you do not need a broker to assist you in selecting particular issues to invest in, then consider a discount brokerage house (one that offers reduced commissions to its customers when they buy and sell secu-rities). There are many fine discount brokers, the biggest being Charles Schwab & Co. Your local newspaper usually carries advertisements for some of the discount brokers throughout the week.

The primary difference between full-service (i.e., Merrill Lynch) and discount brokers is that you are not inundated with all kinds of invest-ment recommendations and you may actually save about 50 percent of the commissions usually charged by a full-service brokerage house. My experience suggests that with a little reading and understanding, you can make investment choices as poorly as some of the professionals, and probably a lot better.

Most stockbrokers participate in a continuing education program, though they are not required to, to maintain their licenses. Many have completed courses for the CFP degree (for certified financial planner). To me, this is a big plus. It means they are continuing to stretch and learn more about the wide world of money. CFPs are required to meet minimal continuing educational hours to maintain the designation.

> Require that the professional advisor you work with *put recommendations in writing*. Once you commit, begin a paper trail to protect yourself if things go sour. After your meeting (or phone calls), follow up. This is your responsibility—to yourself and to your family.

Let's say your objective is to buy a home within two years. It makes sense to tell your broker or financial planner that in writing, that you want nothing long term. Short-term bonds or no-load mutual funds may be the best fit. What is not a fit is placing your moneys in something like a limited partnership, an investment that could take ten years plus to realize any money. In addition, keep a journal of meetings and phone conversations. Note what was recommended and what authorizations you gave. *If* you ever have a complaint, you have records to back you up.

> Read all your mail relating to money matters when it arrives.

Don't ignore or save for future reading *anything* that comes from an advisor or broker. Every transaction, buying or selling, is confirmed with a receipt or confirmation slip. Keep your eyes out for "S" and "U" on these slips for trades. "S" means solicited; "U" means unsolicited. If your brokerage firm sends you a transaction marked "U" and you did not ask the broker to buy or sell, you should call the broker. If you see an error, get it straightened out immediately or you may be stuck if there is trouble later—trouble meaning that the transaction may be inappropriate for you and should not have been done. This will be your legal "C.Y.A."

REGISTERED INVESTMENT ADVISORS OR INVESTMENT COUNSELORS

Registered Investment Advisers (RIAs) or investment counselors are registered with the Securities Exchange Commission (SEC) for the purpose of administering investment-related advice. Unless an individual or group has been in the investment advisory field for a number of years, I would not attach a lot of significance to this particular license. It does not require the testing or knowledge that other licenses do, and it is not difficult to obtain this registration.

If you are adept at filling out government forms (which, I will admit, does deserve some commendation) and can come up with the required fee, there is a high probability that you will be able to obtain a license as a Registered Investment Adviser, as 98 percent of the individuals who apply for it do.

> The bottom line is to check out your financial advisors. Don't work with someone just because they are nice.

RIAs don't get commissions on anything you put money into—at least, they shouldn't. They don't work for free. Ask how they are compensated. Most charge either a fee based on a percentage of the dollar amount of assets managed or a fixed annual fee. Whatever it is, this fee means that your investment portfolio earnings must exceed the cost of their service *plus* the cost of inflation and *then some* to gain any ground. Make sure you get a copy of their track record for a minimum of five years.

ATTORNEYS

The attorney you work with should be a specialist, meaning that a minimum of 50 percent of his or her practice is dedicated to the field that you are seeking advice in—be it business, real estate, estate planning, divorce, or employment. If it is a tax attorney you are looking for, I would raise the bar—75 percent of the practice should be in this area.

One of the important things to find out when you make an appointment with an attorney is whether you will be charged for the initial interview. If you aren't, and it becomes clear that you are really there to obtain free information, the interview will probably be ended. Attorney fees vary in quite a spread—from less than $100 an hour to several hundreds per hour.

Attorney's fees can mushroom by their adding on charges, sometimes excessive, for copying and phone calls. Make sure you clarify exactly how, what, and when you are charged. I would encourage you to formulate a list of questions you want to ask before you get on the phone or have an office appointment. Forget about being social; it's your nickel that will pay for all the niceties.

CERTIFIED PUBLIC ACCOUNTANTS OR ENROLLED AGENTS

Most of us are obligated to pay taxes. What you don't want is someone who merely acts as a bookkeeper. An enrolled agent is someone who has passed a series of extensive tests that allows them to represent clients before the IRS. Most enrolled agents are former IRS employees. Many are quite good and can be helpful to you in routine tax matters.

Certified Public Accountants (CPAs) have a great deal more training than an enrolled agent—and will charge you for it. CPAs are not all alike. Some function more as bookkeepers, whereas others are entrenched in complicated tax law. Don't assume that any CPA will understand a complex tax deal that relates to property or investments that you own. A good question for you to ask in an interview is, "How many of your clients that you presently work with have situations similar to mine?"

> Anytime that assets are to be sold or distributed, the tax consequences must be considered and planned *before* you take any action.

Find a CPA whose practice is mainly with individuals like you. When you interview him or her, ask how he or she is compensated. Ask if any of the individual's clients have been audited or get large refunds. If a high percentage are audited, does it mean that the CPA is too aggressive, interpreting the tax laws very loosely, or does it mean that the majority of the clientele are more prone to being audited (i.e., physicians, dentists, and the self-employed). If refunds are hefty, why is that? Withholding should be changed to reflect a decrease in tax obligations each year. Ask if he or she will stand by you in the case of an audit and appear on your behalf.

> Your accountant or tax advisor should query you as to your anticipated income, determine what expenses could be tax deductible, and advise you of appropriate W-4 changes on an annual basis. If not, you are being misrepresented.

CPAs are required to take continuing education courses for tax-planning updates. Expect to be charged $65 to $200 plus an hour for their services.

Insurance Agents

If you own a home, rent a home or an apartment, have kids, are married, or drive a car, you should have insurance. Some agents offer and sell all types of insurance (life, casualty, health, long-term, and disability), and others sell only one type, such as life. Some agents sell policies from several companies; others, from only one company.

Insurance agents who consider themselves professionals offer an alphabet soup of designations—CLU (Certified Life Underwriter), ChFC (Chartered Financial Consultant), or LUTCF (Life Underwriter Training Council Fellowship). Each designation represents varying levels of training and testing, which is good for you. It means that he or she is committed to the profession and has been in it for many years.

You may come across insurance-sales people who are primarily salesmen or saleswomen, not insurance professionals. Six months ago, they may have been selling real estate or cars.

> Of all the financial professionals, insurance has one of the single highest turnover rates. Approximately 90 percent drop out of selling their first year—that's why you want the financial professional in your life to have been in his or her profession at least five years.

When you are purchasing insurance, shop around. For example, check the most recent *Consumer Reports* ratings (your local library is a good resource here) on insurance companies or go to its Web site, *www. consumerreports.com*. Bear in mind that not all insurance companies are equal in service and coverage. And you do not always get more coverage for more money.

If you are knowledgeable about your life insurance needs, you can let your fingers do the walking for your coverage. In Smart Money Move #3, several companies were identified that sell low-cost insurance. Review the section and make a few phone calls.

Insurance professionals usually get paid by commission—when they sell you a policy. Throughout your money life, you will need a variety of insurance. Be prepared to shop and compare and, at times, to switch companies. Do not buy policies and stick them in the drawer, forgetting what you have until you think you may need to file a claim.

REAL ESTATE AGENTS

When buying a home, you will most likely use a real estate agent to represent you. If you are buying commercial real estate (apartments and other buildings), you should use an agent who specializes in commercial real estate, not residential. When buying or selling your personal residence, go with someone who knows your area and specializes in residential properties.

Real estate agents are required to take continuing education courses. They work on commission and most are willing to negotiate their fee, especially if they represent you on both sides of a transaction—buying and selling.

CERTIFIED DIVORCE PLANNERS

In 1998 I identified a new financial professional—the Certified Divorce Planner, also known as a CDP. As of this writing, there are some 400 individuals in the United States who have that designation. They are trained in a multitude of areas of divorce, including the tax consequences of property divisions, payment and receipt of alimony and household support, marital property, and pension and retirement accounts. If the courtroom looks like a possibility, a CDP can be an important member of your divorce advisory team and make a difference financially when the divorce is over.

To find a CDP in your area, contact the Institute of Certified Divorce Planners (ICDP) in Boulder, Colorado, at 800-875-2760. Its Web site is *www.InstituteCDP.com*.

"PRO"CEED THROUGH THE MONEY MAZE

I've been leading money workshops since the early 1970s. One of my standard recommendations is to attend the free seminars that are offered by brokerage firms. The primary purpose is to pitch a specific product and get *you* as a client. The product might be mutual funds, retirement planning, what's ahead in the economy, real estate opportunities, the Roth IRA; it could even be about stocks in general. I attended one cosponsored by a broker and a mutual fund company last year. The food was good, and I learned about a new investment designed for parents who are planning for their children's college costs.

Thousands of new clients are obtained this way every year. At the seminar the representatives of the brokerage house will often ask you to supply your name and address as well as day and evening phone numbers where you can be reached. A broker may then call and encourage you to invest your money according to his or her recommendation. You don't have to give your name and address if you are asked—it's up to you. If you do, expect a phone call within a few days from one of the brokers who attended the session.

A good broker will call you within a week unless he or she discovers that the numbers you gave were phony and their lead is invalid. It is highly improbable that you will hear any further from them unless you are listed in the phone book. Is this misleading? Not in my book—where does it say that you have to submit to a "sales pitch"?

After you have attended several such seminars, you will begin to notice similarities. Each type of investment has some common goals, and these seminars will be a learning tool that can help you find your own "right fit." And if you are like a lot of people you learn faster in an interactive environment. Reading is a self-discipline that comes easily for some, but is boring to many others.

You will hear terms that may seem like a foreign language: depreciation, accelerated depreciation, recapture, cost basis, phantom income, minimum tax bracket, acquisition costs, speculation, high risk, raw land and developmental property, commercial buildings, triple net lease, adjusted basis, leverage, and nonrecourse loans. Relax—these terms will not gobble you up. As they become more familiar, you will find that the money-maze jargon can actually be fun!

Every community offers programs on money management and investment. You just have to start probing who's offering what. Typically, most community colleges offer investment courses as a one- or two-day class. They are taught by qualified professionals and cover such topics as financial planning, beginning investments, and the stock market. What's good about these classes is that they can introduce the financial jargon in a nonintimidating environment. If the class offers lots of new data, you may not be able to absorb it all. There's nothing wrong with taking a repeat course.

Your education in financial matters should also include a close look at how you spend your own money. The cash-flow chart in the preceding chapter gives you a good idea of where your dollars go. Most of us are spenders rather than savers or planners. Many of us seem to think that we are immortal. But as my Aunt Betty always said, "There are three sure things—death, taxes, and arthritis." Today Aunt Betty might add "Good money management just might help you face all three."

What else should you keep abreast of? Everything else. By this I mean local and world events, conditions, trends, and changes. Impossible? Not really. Most of us read a daily newspaper. Continue to do so, but in a more analytical manner than you may have done in the past. Take note of such things as declining interest rates, devaluation of the dollar, crop failures, and the toppling of governments. These events, although they may seem irrelevant to you on a day-to-day basis, will affect your investments.

> Unfortunately, in this day and age it is no longer enough to be a "good and thrifty individual." Since you have come this far in establishing financial objectives and developing money sense, it would be foolish not to use all the available sources to monitor and implement your strategy.

Specialists are no replacement for your own hard-won understanding and autonomous financial control. But you do still need the help of those who know their way through the refinements that mark today's financial, legal, and tax worlds.

SUMMING UP—ADVISORS ARE PLENTIFUL

Most women don't need a gaggle of experts. Before you rush off to hire any and all, sharpen your pencil. Do your homework. Gather any data that will be beneficial for the advisor before you make your first appointment. Previous tax returns, cash flow and net worth statements, brokerage and investment-related statements that summarize your investments and what your cost basis was, life and disability insurance policies—any documents that will tell the advisor where you presently are.

It is not uncommon for women to be more loyal to money advisors—bankers, lawyers, accountants, realtors, insurance agents, stockbrokers, and financial planners—than to their own money. There are key differences between men and women when it comes to money advisors.

- Women tend to form a type of friendship with their advisors, not wanting to terminate the relationship even if there are signs of poor advice or management.

- Some women too willingly abdicate financial decisions to someone else. They rarely follow up on what is suggested or done to their accounts. This is a direct result of influences from their upbringing.

- Family members and friends are sometimes quite vocal in their level of "expertise." Giving in is sometimes easier than standing one's ground and learning more about a situation or handling one's own money. Don't follow the easiest course. Lots of folks spout off advice, rarely following it themselves. Sometimes, controlling you is their real motive.

- Women, more than men, get caught up in scams, especially as they get older. Scam artists come out of the woodwork after there has been a publicized death (they read the obituary pages). More on this will be covered in chapter 9.

Being successful throughout the money mazes of life requires a commitment to monitor information, develop an independent judgment based on that information, and stay involved. It's a Smart Money Move.

---

10 Smart Money Questions to Ask Advisors

When it comes to building a financial team, you want to make sure that your players are at the top of their respective fields. Ask the questions here that fit the professionals you use.

1. **Do you work with other professionals or are you a sole practitioner?** No one person can know all the aspects of financial issues, tax laws, retirement issues, or whatever. Most people who work alone scramble to keep up with any changes in their field. Associates and partners can fill in the gaps.

2. **How is your personal portfolio doing?** Any CFP, stockbroker, or financial advisor of any sort who recommends how to invest *your* money ought to be investing their own, don't you think? I do. It may be a tad touchy to ask someone about his or her personal investments, but wouldn't you be more comfortable with someone who had a successful investment history rather than someone who scrambles to pay the rent each month? I have one friend who routinely asks the men and women who call him to solicit his investment account to send him a copy of their investment

statements so that he can see how they are doing. He tells them that if they outperform what he is personally doing, he will open an account. No one has ever taken him up on his offer!

3. **Can I have references?** Most professionals are happy to provide names of current clients they work with—of course, they should not give out names and phone numbers without first getting the client's permission. Ask for referrals who have been with them at least three years.

4. **How do you charge?** Pay close attention here. Some will charge by the hour, some by a percentage of assets managed, some by commission only, some by a combination method, and others won't charge (bankers are salaried).

5. **How long have you been in your practice and advising clients?** The only answer that you want to hear is a minimum of five years.

6. **Have you made errors in advising clients in the past?** Everyone makes mistakes, including financial advisors. If someone says, "No, I've never made any errors," watch to see if her nose grows. Take a pass and keep shopping. If she or he fesses up, ask what they were and what was learned; then you be the judge.

7. **Have you ever had any complaints filed against you?** You can check with the National Association of Security Dealers (NASD—there's a site on the Internet) or the Securities and Exchange Commission (SEC) for securities complaints. For real estate and insurance, check with your state departments that cover those areas. A word of caution: when it comes to money and investments, some people sue if something does not work out as expected—it doesn't matter if the advisor didn't cause it. More financial advisors than not have been sued by a disgruntled former client looking for a deep pocket from which to get their money back. It happens.

8. **Where do you get your money advice from?** This question will catch them off guard. Do they just recite whatever their company tells them to or do they actively seek other sources?

9. **What publications do you read, listen to, or view on a regular basis?** They should be more than *Time* and *Newsweek*. Magazines such as *Money* or *Fortune* and newspapers including the *Wall Street Journal* should head the list. Depending on what associations they belong to, there will be professional trade journals with their memberships. Access to the Internet brings an incredible arsenal of information. Stations, such as CNNfn, CNN, PBS, MSNBC, and CNBC, broadcast business, investment, consumer, legal, and money programs throughout the day.

10. **Do you belong to any professional associations?** Active professionals should belong to associations that enhance their skills and education. You should hear names such as the International Association of Financial Planners or the Institute of Certified Financial Planners, the American Banking Association, a national insurance or real estate association (there are lots of them), or the American Bar Association.

6

Invest for Fun . . . and Profit

I have great news. Women do not make as many "bad" investments as men do. Why? Men are far more inclined to make decisions based on hot tips. They'll follow their cronies—if *they* buy, it must be good. Women rarely do. Women are more inclined to do some probing into an investment opportunity before they commit. Do men know more than women do about how to make it rich quick? Absolutely not . . . but someone said that men somehow should know how to make money in investments.

So, where do you start? I'd suggest on the light side. Don't take a major plunge until you have experience buying and selling stocks or other investments on a money scale that doesn't overwhelm you. There are lots of ways to invest your money. If all of them were identified, this book would have a thousand pages. I'll keep it simple. The most common way you enter the investment arena is through the purchase of individual stocks and mutual funds. We'll explore those together.

If you have an unpleasant experience, which means you lose money, it will influence you for several years to come. Some people have become extremely successful in the stock market, whereas others have been unsuccessful and never recover from the pain. My experience has shown that most have a love-or-hate relationship with the market. They either want to take part in it because they think there is a great potential there or they want nothing to do with it and would rather deal with something they can see and feel, such as real estate or collectibles.

Sooner or later, every investor will probably put some money in the stock market—even though many think of it as a dangerous jungle. They may be right! But investing in stocks of sturdy, growing businesses is one way to help your dollars keep up with or even ahead of recurring inflation. The stock market is to some the symbol of our economic system. It is accessible and, in a sense, it seems downright patriotic to invest in the strength and fortitude of individual American businesses.

> This is an important, big chapter. Be prepared to return to it several times as you invest and reinforce your Smart Money Moves. Keep your Post-its and highlighter handy.

The stock market is a vehicle for growth—especially for the novice or small investor. Although it's true the stock market can be a lucrative investment opportunity, it can also be a bizarre and ephemeral circus, susceptible to whims and emotions—a Las Vegas gambling hall with dozens of glittering games of chance. To invest well in the stock market you must know the risks, the rewards, and the remedies.

TAKING THE PLUNGE

An understanding of the market is basic to understanding our underlying money management system. Also, it happens to be a place where smarts, common sense, and sometimes a little luck can really pay off.

First of all, what is the stock market? Basically, it's where you buy ownership rights in an incorporated business. You do this by buying *common stock* or *shares.* You are not lending money; you are actually buying part of the company. You have a claim on profits and, technically, a say in management and policy. Rarely, however, do stockholders exercise these rights. Most stockholders are realistic and view their role as a passive one.

The value of stock changes constantly. Basically, what it's worth is whatever someone else will pay for it. And that's determined on the stock exchanges, a vast array of markets for stocks and bonds, where they are bought and sold by authorized agents via a stockbroker.

The business of the stock market is conducted on two major national exchanges: the New York Stock Exchange (NYSE) and the American Stock Exchange (AMEX). The NYSE has slightly stricter standards for the companies they list, but both exchanges require proven earnings records and demonstrated financial stability.

There is also an over-the-counter (OTC) market of countless securities not listed on an exchange, but traded among brokers, over the phone, with varying degrees of activity. Over-the-counter stocks are not necessarily riskier. To find quotations for companies listed in the OTC market, you would look in the newspaper under Nasdaq (The National Association of Securities Dealers Automated Quotation System). Many well-known companies have chosen to stay listed in the over-the-counter market rather than trading on the New York Stock Exchange, the American Stock Exchange, or one of the other, much smaller exchanges, such as the Pacific Coast Stock Exchange. Don't feel you have to shy away from a stock just because it's not listed on the "Big Board." Nasdaq is the usual starting point for new companies. The listing requirements (i.e., earnings per share and number of shareholders) are less stringent than the NYSE. Many companies change their affiliation from Nasdaq to the AMEX or NYSE, the primary reason being more prestige.

GROWTH VERSUS INCOME

There are two primary types of stock: growth stocks and income stocks. A growth company often pays little, if any, money in cash dividends. This is because it tends to be a new or small company, which is likely to plow a large share of its earnings back into the company for research and development to achieve growth and expansion. Classic examples are companies in the technology field. A substantial part of their market price represents prospects for the future, rather than their past performance. The value of the *growth stock* itself is expected to rise substantially over the coming years, so you can gain in value without having to pay taxes before you sell.

> Growth stocks are purchased when immediate income is not the goal.

High-yield, or *income, stocks* are just that—stocks that distribute a large portion of the company's profits to stockholders in the form of a cash dividend. Utility stocks fit in here.

Somewhere in the middle of these two are what are known as *blue chip stocks.* These are supposedly conservative, proven stocks, which offer some growth, a respectable dividend, and, hopefully, peace of mind. Many people think of AT&T, IBM, Proctor & Gamble, and Johnson & Johnson as classic examples of blue chip stocks.

Throughout this chapter the concept of "what goes up will come down" is reinforced. These blue chip companies are all well known and managed. Their stock values, however, can be subject to change—some big ones.

THE DOW JONES INDUSTRIAL AVERAGES

Usually, I don't recommend checking on your individual stock holdings on a daily basis, but a daily check of the Dow Jones Industrial Average can help you keep abreast of the overall thrust of the market. Exact it is not! It consists of only thirty stocks and is not updated regularly to parallel the various growth industries as they emerge.

The most recent changes to the Dow Jones Industrial Averages occurred in 1997 when four companies were replaced: Travelers Group for Westinghouse Electric Corp., Hewlett-Packard Co. for Texas Inc., Johnson & Johnson for Bethlehem Steel Corp., and Wal-Mart Stores Inc. for Woolworth Corp. Changes are not made every year, but when they are, they are usually done to reflect the current business environment.

By scanning stock quotations, you can get a good idea of what went on the day before and try to spot patterns correlating with other news items that may influence the market. Here's an example of a quotation for JC Penney and an explanation of how to read it:

Sample Stock Quotation
September 16, 1998

1		2	3	4	5	6	7	8	9	10	11
52 weeks					%	PE	100				Net
H	L	Stock	Symbol	Div.	yld.	ratio	Sales	High	Low	Close	Change
78¾	48⅝♣	Penney JC	JCP	2.18	4.2	26	5908	52⁷/₁₆	51½	51¹³/₁₆	-⅛

1. In the last fifty-two weeks the stock has traded as high as 78-3/4 per share and as low as 48-5/8 per share. The shamrock (♣) means that financial reports are available for the noted company through the *Wall Street Journal.*
2. The name of the company or stock, commonly abbreviated, is given here.
3. The symbol used on the stock exchange to identify the company.

---

4. The amount of the dividend paid per share per year.
5. The percentage of the current price per share return that annual dividends paid represent.
6. The PE ratio represents the price of a share divided by the earnings per share for a twelve-month period. In our illustration, JC Penney is selling for $51-13/16 per share, and the stated PE ratio is 26. If you divide 51-13/16 by 26, the result is approximately $1.99, which represents earnings for the past fifty-two weeks.
7. Sales are reported in 100s, so multiply 5,908 by 100, arriving at 590,800 as the number of shares traded on September 16, 1998.
8. Stock traded as high as $52-7/16 per share during the day.
9. Stock traded as low as $51-1/2 during the day.
10. Stock closed at $51-13/16 per share.
11. Stock closed 1/8 ($0.125) of a point less than the preceding day's close.

Source: The Wall Street Journal

CHOOSING A STOCK

You have undoubtedly heard stories about how choosing stocks as if you were playing darts often produces better results than consulting with the most reputable stockbroker. In truth, some luck seems to be involved, but logic and reasoning also are. Over the years I have become convinced that there are plenty of areas where any novice investor willing to do some serious homework can outperform the vast majority of professionals. This conviction is based on working with innumerable uninformed, supposedly unsophisticated women. Consider this one an example.

When I was a stockbroker, I once conducted a weekend class at the University of California at Santa Cruz, which some forty women attended. Those who did not live in the immediate area stayed overnight in the dorms. A few days before the classes began, *Business Week* magazine published an article covering the fast-food industry. The first day of class I presented the market and its various options. I presented some simple rules for evaluating the information available to every investor considering a stock purchase. I firmly believe that the last thing any of us really needs to be successful is "inside" information.

I showed the group how to determine book values, evaluate percentages, compare the market and book-value increases, and even how simple it is to determine the price-earnings ratio.

Of the companies presented, I chose several that had ratings from *Value Line Investment Survey* and presented them in the afternoon. *Value Line* is one of the top-rated advisories and is available at no cost at most brokerage houses and libraries and for an annual fee to individuals. Samples will be used as illustrations later in this chapter. I find the publication's information an invaluable tool.

The women were asked to evaluate each of the stocks and pick the one that seemed to have the best chance of increasing in value, using the standards I had described. What were those standards? Nothing very complicated; they involved merely going back over the last five years to determine the percentages of increases or decreases that had occurred from year to year in earnings per share, book values, price-earnings ratios, capital expenditures, sales per share, profit margin, and other areas I had pointed out. This assignment kept class members busy all evening.

The following morning they returned to class and presented their choices. Almost all had been able to select the stock that seemed most appealing. That stock was all but unknown in the early 1980s. Today its shares are owned by major institutions all over the world and by women such as you and me. In the year after the class, in fact, the stock had increased significantly in price. It showed itself to be aggressive and forward-looking. The market appreciated the vision of its management. Its subsequent growth was no surprise to the stock market neophytes who met that weekend in Santa Cruz. The stock? Wendy's, named after the daughter of owner Dave Thomas.

What I taught these women was quite simple. I showed them some of the essentials to look for in a stock, but I also showed them how to apply common sense in evaluating a possible stock purchase.

Every major journey must have its beginning. It usually isn't sufficient for a stock or a group of companies to be riding a wave that never breaks. Remember, all waves crash, and when a stock climbs quickly in value, often it's the first to fall, especially when there is a vogue or fad involved.

The only times fortunes and empires are built on fads are when those who trade or invest in them can get out before everyone else gets in. You are looking for the next L'eggs Panty Hose, the vision of retailer Nordstrom or Microsoft, and the savvy of shoe producers Nike and Reebok.

If you sight something you feel is a possible trend, determine who produces the product or provides the service and which exchange their stock is traded on, if it is. The next step is to tune in—learn to examine the key indicators of the company's potential.

Balance Sheet

Current assets of a company should outnumber its liabilities by at least two to one. The greater the ratio in favor of assets, the better for the stockholder. Of course, there are exceptions to every rule. Companies in the high technology areas often require a higher ratio of assets because they expend so much up front in research and development. On the other hand, railroads, airlines, and utilities often operate successfully with less than a two-to-one ratio.

Another ratio to look at closely is the *quick ratio,* or acid test. That's determined by taking all the current assets on the balance sheet and deducting inventory. The remaining number is then compared to current liabilities. The ratio you're looking for is one to one. Bankers look closely at this ratio. The reason? If inventory can't be sold, they want to make sure there's sufficient cash available to meet the ongoing payables and debt requirements of the company.

You need to think like a banker. There's nothing worse than yesterday's popular product that will never sell again.

Earnings Record

A company's earnings should either be constant over the past several years or show continuing increase. There will always be peaks and valleys, especially if the economy goes through a whopping recession. A speculative investor, someone who is often going for an aggressive growth position, looks for companies that have high ups and low downs, hoping to find and hit the right pattern. For you, as a first-time investor, this strategy should be avoided like the plague.

Dividend Record

If you're buying a stock for income purposes, make sure you research the company's dividend payments for the last ten years. They need to have been paid consistently, with an increase per annum over that period. Don't give up on a stock that has had one bad year. Companies often do. Again, if you see a downturn, look at what happened to the overall economy during that specific time. Even a properly managed company can suffer during a downturn in the national economy.

Caution: In the 1990s, the granddaddy of car manufacturers did the unthinkable—it cut its dividend. General Motors had no choice: it had been hemorrhaging for years. Yet, most investors were shocked—caught off guard. This appalls me. The negative news about GM and the auto industry in general was well-known. The cutbacks and millions of dollars in losses had been front page news for a long time. The obvious response, much earlier, would have been to sell your stock. After all, earnings losses were building year after year. In GM's case, the losses amounted to billions of dollars.

GM had been one of the "orphan and widow" stocks, one that every major financial institution owned. Yet many stockholders didn't sell until . . . the layoffs and the losses were history. By then, a substantial decline in market value had occurred, and the dividend had to be reduced significantly. Those who lived on a fixed income were stunned by their loss. I don't know why—the news had been in the press for months that there were not sufficient earnings to cover dividend obligations. All one had to do was pick up a newspaper once a month and read the business section.

> If you buy stocks for their dividend yield, keep them only if the total of the stated dividends paid is less than 50 percent of the stock's earnings. The exception would be utility companies. They operate differently from other industries. Their revenues come from a captured customer—a customer who can't call up XYZ company for gas and electricity if rates are too high with the ABC company. The result is that the utility can pay out a greater percentage of earnings to shareholders. No more than 75 percent of their earnings should be paid out for dividends.

PRICE-EARNINGS RATIO

Computing the price-earnings (PE) ratio is easily done by dividing the current market price of a stock by the last-known earnings per share. This figure is given in most stock advisories, and it certainly is in your daily newspaper. If a stock sells at $40 a share and has earnings of $5 a share, then its price-earnings ratio is ($40 ÷ $5). Normally, the higher the PE ratio is, the more risk is involved. The stock quotation pages in your newspaper routinely carry the PE ratio, so you don't need to be a math whiz.

PRICING REALITY

Stocks are usually priced for a reason—good or poor management, growth possibilities, outside influences such as government regulation, inconsistency in marketing, pricing, and policy. There are a whole variety of reasons. Your job is to probe and find out what some of those reasons may be.

When you finally have these numbers, it's critical to apply your common sense and overall perceptions of current and future trends. Look at a company's line of products in relationship to consumer tastes and preferences. Keep in mind any information you've collected from outside sources, such as magazines or newspapers, that could influence the price of the stock.

COMPARISON SHOPPING

When you're considering a company for investment purposes, it makes sense to compare that company with others in the same field. Compare the stock's specific averages, increases and decreases in earnings per share, net worth, dividends, revenues per share, capital spending per share, operating profit, and working capital.

Much of this information can be found in the resource I mentioned earlier, the *Value Line Investment Survey.* Look at the chart of a company that may be familiar to you such as Nordstrom, Inc., a specialty department store located in several states. Nordstrom is famous for its customer service—all personnel have the authority to do whatever it takes to keep the customer happy. In addition to the Nordstrom department stores, the company owns The Rack Off, Plane Two, and Last Chance stores.

Nordstrom began as a shoe store in Seattle, Washington, and it has since expanded to incorporate all the clothing types carried by most top-end retail stores. Its management will not tolerate rudeness to the customer or inattention to work. The store courts and successfully keeps its customers for the rest of their shopping lives.

Today, women (and men) covet the "Nordstrom experience"—the customer is truly queen or king.

Nordstrom *Value Line Investment Survey*

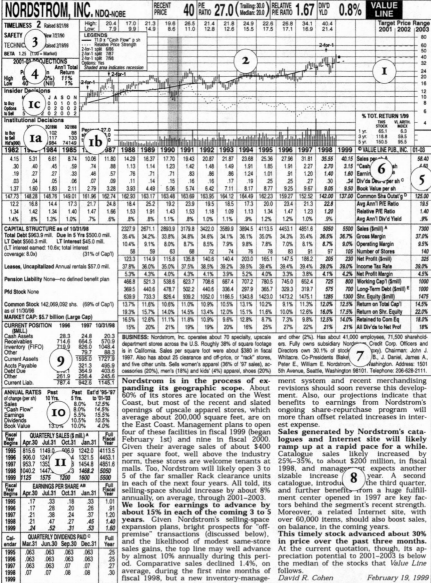

Note the key areas in the chart, which I have highlighted for you:

1. This chart illustrates that Nordstrom has fluctuated in price, beginning in 1986 (the stock sold before 1986; it just isn't reflected here due to space limitation) with a trading range less than $6 per share and going to a high of $32 per share. As you can see, the stock has had some price swings.

   1a. If you had purchased this stock in the 1980s, you would not have seen much action in the price through 1985. Certainly this is one you would not have made your fortune on. On the other hand, because of the minimal price movement, it is not an investment in which you would have lost your grocery money either.

   1b. The stock moved from $6 per share in 1986 to $20 in 1987, then declined to $8, increased over two years back to $20, declined over the next year to $9, had a few more years of ups and downs, then saw a gradual increase through the 1990s to the stock's quoted price of $32 a share in late August of 1998—a handsome increase for those who were patient.

   1c. Nordstrom stock is owned by many banks and mutual funds.

2. Nordstrom has had four two-for-one stock splits. The first split was in 1983, followed by 1986, 1987, and 1998. If you had 100 shares in 1983, it would have doubled to 200 in 1986 and doubled again to 400 in 1986, to 800 shares in 1987, and 1,600 shares in 1998!

3. Be aware of the timeliness and safety rankings. Both of these are based on a one-to-five scale, with one being the best. Nordstrom is ranked "two" in timeliness. That means it's above average and its market value is increasing at a greater rate than the overall Dow Jones Industrial Average. Its safety is "three." This is based on the financial position of the company as well as the oscillation of the stock. In other words, you shouldn't lose much sleep over this stock. It's average in movement in relation to the rest of the stock market.

4. Take projections with a grain of salt.

5. The actual financial reports are important. Note the increased sales per share, earnings per share, book value per share, capital spending (if a company is planning any growth, there should always be funds allocated for capital spending), average annual PE ratio, and net profit margins.

6. If you desire income from your investments, note the kind of dividends per share. Nordstrom does not pay much in dividends. It yields about 1 percent. Therefore, if you need income, this is not a stock that will meet your criterion. The amount it pays is minimal, and the company's past history is not to pay out much of earnings to shareholders. You may be thinking, Why would I want this stock if I don't get a return on my investment? Returns are not always measured in dividends. Companies that are growing and expanding, as Nordstrom is, need cash to grow. Growth usually enhances the stock's market price.

7. The center section is important. It tells who the company is, what their major products are, who the CEO (chief executive officer) is, the company locations, and its corporate address and phone number. It often shows a percentage split of revenues per major product line. When you address complaint letters to the CEO, by the way, action usually results.

8. Major information is noted—changes in directions for the company and how the investment community projects these changes. For those of you who are interested in career changes or job repositioning, this is an ideal section to read. Knowing about future products may put you one up in an interview.

9. Current position represents the last two years, as well as the current year, with a breakout of assets and liabilities.

10. This figure represents the annual rates for the past five and ten years on percentages of increases for sales, cash flow, earnings, dividends, and book value. It often includes estimates in increases or decreases for the next period of time.

11. Here you see current financial data on dividends paid, quarterly sales and earnings per share for the preceding four years, as well as estimates for the current year.

12. The company's financial strength is important. If you are conservative, then it makes sense to go with an "A" or better rating. If you are willing to take a little risk and look at companies that may be growth-oriented (such as Nordstrom), turnaround candidates, or fairly new on the investment scene, then a rating of less than "A" may be perfectly all right.

TIME TO PROBE

Let's take a look at an investment in Nordstrom. Let's say that you purchased 100 shares in 1986, prior to its stock split. The stock's price ranged from $6 to $8 per share. If you paid top dollar, your investment for the 100 shares would be $800 plus commission. For illustration purposes, I will ignore commissions.

In 1986 a two-for-one split was declared, increasing your holdings to 200 shares. In 1987 there was another two-for-one split, increasing your shares to 400, in 1998 another. You now own 800 shares of Nordstrom.

In looking at the market value on February 19, 1999 (*The Value Line Survey* date), at $40 a share your overall holdings have appreciated from $800 to $32,000 or a $31,200 profit. Since your initial purchase in 1986, dividends have been paid. Although minimal, Nordstrom has increased its annual dividend every year since 1982. The total amount you have received in dividends for your 800 shares from 1985 through 1998 is $936.

In other words, during the twelve years of holding Nordstrom stock, your money has increased 3,217 percent—not bad indeed. Could you have done better (or worse)? Sure—let's check out Bill Gates's child, Microsoft Corporation.

GEEKS 'R' US—THE MICROSOFT WAY

I won't go through the detail of identifying each of the sections for Microsoft as I did for Nordstrom. You will discover that *The Value Line Survey* is always laid out in the same format. Note the price range of the stock as reflected on the graph, beginning in 1990. Microsoft traded publicly prior to that, but its price was so low that it is off the charts. The date of *The Value Line Survey* is March 5, 1999, when Microsoft closed at $76 per share.

Let's say you bought 100 shares of Microsoft in 1990 just before its first two-for-one split. Your cost would have been approximately $2 per share for a total investment of $200 plus commissions. Microsoft has had six stock splits, four two-for-one and two three-for-two. The total shares you would hold after the seven splits would be 7,200 shares, with a market value of $547,200, a nine-year profit of $547,000. Even better.

Microsoft *Value Line Investment Survey*

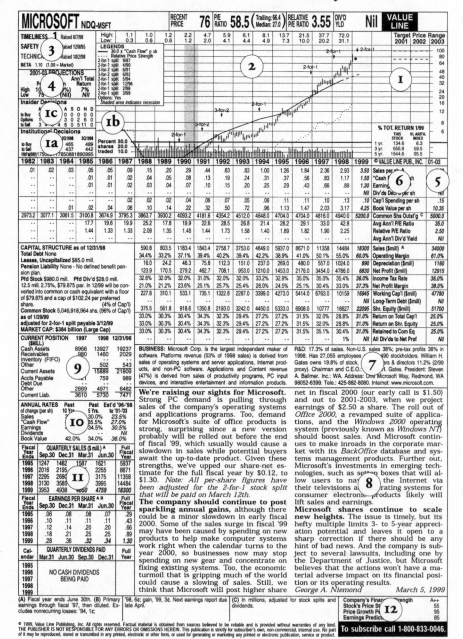

STOCK SPLITS AND DIVIDENDS

For growth, stocks that have a history of paying dividends in stock (not cash), in stock splits, or both ways outperform those that do not. Companies that are aggressively growing can't give cash to shareholders (at least, not much). Instead, additional stock through stock dividends and splits is the preferred method to "reward" stockholders.

WHY STOCKS SPLIT

Let's say you work for a company whose cash is tied up in expansion, research, and development. To keep investors happy the company could give them dividends in the form of more stock, rather than cash. In young companies the practice of giving dividends in the form of the company's stock versus cash dividends is common. And, if you were to look at the fluctuations of their stock prices over the last decade, you would see that some of these stocks had had one or more splits.

If you had shares of a company that elected to have a four-for-one split, it would mean that for every share you had, you would now have four. When a stock splits four for one, it doesn't mean that you have four times the value at the time of the split. You have the *same total* value but four times the number of shares, each of which is one-fourth its value prior to the split.

Let's say that you had 1,000 shares of stock and the stock has appreciated to $50 a share. Your total value is $50,000. Management decides to give a four-for-one split. This means that instead of having 1,000 shares, your shares will increase to 4,000, but the individual value per share will decrease to $12.50, versus the previous $50. Your overall market value is still the same, but you now own more shares.

Why would a company do this? Sometimes it is done for psychological reasons. Many people can't afford to buy 100 shares of stock for $50 a share, a total purchase price of $5,000 plus commission. But they may be able to buy 100 shares at $12.50 a share or a total price of $1,250 plus commission. As more and more people can afford to purchase the stock, there is a general thrust toward buying and accumulation. The result is the company's stock increases in value.

I have seen many people buy 1,000 shares of a stock for a few dollars a share, later accumulating thousands more shares from various stock dividends or splits. And I am never surprised when these shares continue to appreciate to as high a per-share level as they had traded prior to their splits.

The two potential negatives here are that you might have all your eggs in one basket, which is never a good position to be in, and you might hold such a sizable portion that, if you elected to sell all the shares at one time, you could actually (because of the size of your sale) force down the price. It is usually not a good idea to have many shares in a company that has only a few thousand shareholders. Your selling could cause a decline; if you decided to purchase, you could force the price up a little. Be careful here. When you win, it is absolutely wonderful. But when you lose, ouch. Patience can pay off. Sticking your neck out can pay enormous rewards. If you do, however, take the time to evaluate the risk and rewards of anything that beckons your money.

SPOTTING WINNERS

You may be thinking, "The stocks you have illustrated have already made their profits. Where am I going to find one that has such huge growth?" My response is open your eyes and ears. Pay attention. What products do you use? Your friends use? Your employer? What seems great, not just OK? The hot product of 1998 was the new drug Viagra. Pfizer, which produced it, saw its stock value increase by 50 percent within a few months.

Was this a *big* secret? No. Information about drug testing was reported in newspapers and magazines two years prior. With that information, you could have made a decision. First, would you think desirable a drug that reduces male impotency? "I don't know" may be your response. OK; probe some. Ask a few questions. Start with your own doctor—is impotency a problem for a lot of men? Any guess at the percentage of male population? If you were married or in a relationship, you could have asked your spouse or partner to consider if impotency was a problem whether he would take a pill to eliminate it.

With just those few questions, I would suspect that you would have known that there was a market demand for the drug. You could have even called Pfizer's headquarters in New York and asked its PR department what projections the company managers saw for the drug or called a stock brokerage, such as Merrill Lynch, and asked if its drug analysts had any information. Then, there's the Internet. A tap into the health-care fields could have revealed sources to start tracking.

How do you spot potential winners? Look at the types of business they do. Are they aggressive in their marketing? How often do they successfully bring in new products? Are they appealing to the baby boom generation? Do they get written up in the newspapers or magazines? Do they produce a product you can't buy because the stores can't keep it in stock? Or is it one no one asks for? These are the key questions that need to be addressed.

If you elect to participate in the stock market, consider placing your dollars with young companies that appear to have great growth potential. Keep in mind that the old rules of supply and demand will always apply.

My point here is that identifying and selecting stocks is not for the "pros" only. I have believed since the 1970s that you can do far better on your own if you are willing to do a little homework. Are you?

A TIME TO SELL

I have already emphasized that timing is all important in buying stocks. It is equally important in selling stocks. One of the mistakes stock market investors make is to purchase a stock, put it in a drawer, and forget about it. Or worse, they actually do notice their stocks dropping week after week but they decide to wait until it "comes up again," to at least the original investment cost before selling.

Beware of becoming sentimental about your stock. You should have an expectation—a goal—for every investment. Once you have reached that goal, don't wait around hoping to make an even bigger "killing." Conversely, don't stay too long with a stock that has begun to falter while other stocks are prospering. While you may opt to wait and see what the management of a young, aggressive company can accomplish in growth, remember there's always a right time to sell a stock. Even if you lose some money, you can always deduct the loss on your tax return.

I am not advocating the practice of some brokers who roll or turn your account just to get commissions. I do advocate watching your stocks. Watch the overall performance of your portfolio, use your intuition, but remember that intuition is for the most part just a product of experience and observation. There is a limit to every rising stock. Unfortunately, there is no limit on a falling one until you get down to zero.

When I buy, I set a goal for upside growth. I also set a downside. The rule of thumb I use for taking a profit, or a loss, is this: If an investment declines 20 percent, it's sold. If it increases to the upside goal, let's say double, I ask one question: *If I had more money to invest, would I buy this company at the present price?* If the answer is yes, I stay with it. If it's maybe, I sell half and let the remainder of my money stay in it. If the answer is no, I sell.

Are there times when I sell too soon? Yes. Are there times that I thank my lucky stars that I bailed out? You bet. The bottom line is that I miss some terrific rebounds and I miss some incredible dives. What I have is a plan. So should you.

> Profits are like the fruit on a tree. If you don't pick them when they are ripe, they fall and rot.

Letting go of cash, and possibly tying money up for an indefinite period of time to make more money (and sometimes lose some) may create high levels of anxiety. Investing takes time and patience. My rule for you when it comes to investing is to wait until you have your "liquidity fund" in place. The only exception is when you are able to participate in one of the many types of retirement and income deferral possibilities, such as 401(k) programs, tax-sheltered annuities at work, or an IRA.

INVESTMENT CLUBS

One way to put your toe in the water and have some fun is through an investment club. I invest on my own, and I'm a member of a club that gets together on the third Monday night of every month. Read on. . . .

If you believe in sharing information, an investment club may be a great way for you to enter the wide world of investing. Most clubs start with a group of friends, coworkers, or neighbors who have a common interest— investing in the stock market. Moneys are pooled, and research and information are shared. Some clubs are small; others have twenty to thirty members. There is one sure thing about investment clubs: you definitely will not be alone when it comes time to make an investment decision.

BOOK IT

One of the greatest testimonials for the "club" strategy is the example set by the enormously successful Beardstown Ladies Investment Club. The *New York Times* best seller *The Beardstown Ladies' Common-Sense Investment Guide* trumpets the fact that *anyone* who is willing to do her homework (get information on companies and products they make) can outshine the pros.

Since their club started in 1983, each of its sixteen members has paid in the monthly pledge of $25 for additional stock investments. How did they do? Not bad. Originally it was reported that they averaged over 20 percent per year since they began. A few years after their first book came out, it was discovered that their returns were less than initially reported, an error in their math calculations. What did they buy? Any stocks they bought had to show growth potential. *Earning income* was not the primary goal—*growth* was.

> Investment clubs are terrific places to brainstorm with other members about products they are buying. If some members have small children or grandchildren, ask what toys, TV shows, and movies are hot. Can stock be bought in the companies that produce them? Spread research assignments around to different members.

From these possibilities club members select companies they understand, those they know from use of the company's products, and companies that treat their employees ethically. They are also advocates of Business 101: Supply and Demand. If they as consumers experience delays in obtaining merchandise, they know it is because there is (1) no demand, no stocking of inventory, or (2) a high demand, with inventory flying off the shelves.

Most clubs have a monthly financial requirement. For example, each member initially puts $100 in the kitty and pledges an additional $25 each month. The group decides, after a committee or individuals present companies for consideration, to buy so many shares of a stock or fund. Selling stocks is also done by consensus. Over a period of time, more shares can be purchased and sold. Investment choices are made by popular vote for all buys and sells. The real fun is the competition in finding just the right stock for the group and then selling the other members on its merits.

If you have an interest in starting a club, contact the National Association of Investors Corporation at P.O. Box 220, Royal Oak, MI 48068 or at 711 W. Thirteen Mile Rd., Madison Heights, MI 48071; you can also call 248-583-6242 for an information packet. Many thousands of people belong to investment clubs; most are women. There are more than 8,000 clubs in America. Many belong to the National Association of Investment Clubs, whose dues are $30 per club, plus $10 per member per year. In return, NAIC will send members the *Better Investing* magazine. This is in addition to the partnership agreement and general information on how to form the club and set up accounting procedures.

The net result is that you learn a lot about the stock market without feeling intimidated by your lack of experience as you are learning. Many clubs invite local stockbrokers and financial planners to speak at their meetings.

Investment clubs may be a great way to put your toe in the stock market's waters. There are some wonderful success stories of investment choices—choices made by women such as yourself. The great majority of them had little knowledge of the stock market when they started. They have fun learning and making money together.

MUTUAL FUNDS—SOMETHING FOR EVERYONE

Mutual funds are one of the easiest investment doors to enter with minimal dollars. The definition of a mutual fund is quite simple: it is a pooled investment in a large number of companies, either their stocks, bonds, or a mixture. It is an investment cooperative wherein your stock represents a share in a large portfolio of diverse individual investment vehicles. The decision to buy a mutual fund can be equally easy. Many investors buy into a fund solely because it does represent many companies. It's one way to achieve diversification.

Today almost a trillion dollars have been invested in thousands of mutual funds by millions of investors such as you. These funds can simplify your investment strategies. You do, though, need to know how they work.

When you stick with a family of funds, record keeping is simplified. The fund does most of the work for you. Fund families always have a money market fund within each family. With a phone call you can say, "Sell my shares and put the funds into your money market fund to earn interest."

DIVERSIFICATION AND PROTECTION GO HAND IN HAND

An old adage in the money game is, "When in doubt, diversify, diversify, diversify." The importance of this cannot be overstated, for diversification, or hedging, offers significant protection during uncertain and changing financial times.

Large-scale stock market investors don't entrust all their capital to a few securities. They diversify by carefully selecting a broad range of stocks. Many even include mutual funds within their portfolios. Medium-sized investors are partial to the planned diversification of mutual funds. The smaller investor usually hasn't the capital to buy stock in several companies, but a mutual fund allows her to invest a small amount of money in a large number of different securities.

Many funds allow initial investments as low as $50 if you agree for the fund to automatically withdraw the $50 from your bank each month. Some funds to check out include Janus, 800-525-3713; Twentieth Century, 800-345-2021; and Neuberger & Berman, 800-877-9700.

If you have kids, this is a great way to seed their college education accounts. You can start an educational IRA with a maximum contribution of $500 per year. There are no tax deductions, but there are benefits. When you begin to withdraw funds for educational purposes, anything you withdraw is nontaxable. All growth and income is tax free. That's a Smart Money Move.

DO AS THE EXPERTS DO

Another related advantage to mutual funds is expertise. For busy women who haven't the time or skill to study and pick their own stocks, mutual funds offer professional management. It is not only acceptable, it is also often wise to rely on other people.

Most mutual management teams, by and large, successfully follow consistent investment strategies based on extensive research. But funds, like any other stock, need to be watched because the fund managers decide when and where to trade securities. Sometimes management personnel or strategy changes and the results may not be what you want.

Beyond watching the funds progress, there is little else you really have to do once you buy in. The fund you choose will give you the option of regular cash payments or automatic reinvestment of your earnings. They even do the paperwork needed for the IRS.

OPEN VERSUS CLOSED

There are two types of mutual funds. An *open-end fund* has an infinite number of shares. When more money is put into the fund, more shares are created. Open-end shares are traded at a price determined by the *net asset value* (NAV) of the fund. Thus, the price is a direct reflection of the performance of that fund and the performance of the different stocks within that fund. It is determined every day based on the market value of the stocks or bonds owned. You can cash in holdings in open-end funds for their underlying asset value at a moment's notice. Your check for the proceeds will be in the mail within seven days.

Closed-end funds have a limited number of shares that are traded on the market, their price being determined by supply and demand. Once a closed-end fund is fully funded, no new moneys can be added from investors. The only source of "new" moneys the manager can invest is using the profits from stocks and bonds that are in the fund's portfolio.

Each business day, the total value of all the fund's investments are divided by the number of shares outstanding. This creates the net asset value per share. But here's the catch-22. The NAV may not be what the fund sells for. Instead, it's a supply and demand situation, just as with regular stocks that trade. At times the fund may trade for more than the NAV—this is called trading at a premium. If the fund sells below the NAV, then it trades at a discount. Closed-end fund shares must be sold on an exchange, like ordinary stock. Their shares are as liquid as the open-end funds.

Closed-end funds are purchased through a broker, a discount broker, or a financial planner. This means that whoever handles the transaction gets paid. You might think that by contacting the fund directly, you can save the commission. Wrong. It is either absorbed by the company or they may "place" your purchase with a favored broker.

Reading the values or quotes in your newspaper is not difficult. Below is a reprint of closing quotations for two of the Janus Funds, Mercury and Worldwide, dated September 16, 1998, which reflects how the funds did the day before.

NAV[3]	Net chg[4]	Fund name[1]	YTD% '98 ret[5]	Max init chg[2]	Exp ratio
19.83	+0.21	Mercury	+20.2	0.00	1.14
41.92	+0.22	Wrld W	+11.0	0.00	1.24

1. Note: Wrld W. This is an abbreviation for WorldWide Fund. The Mercury Fund is spelled out.

2. No commission is charged directly to the investor. Instead the management charges administrative expenses. These are reflected within the expense ratio to annual expenses.

3. The net asset value (NAV) is determined at the closing of each business day. NAV is the per-share value calculated by dividing the value of the fund by the number of shares outstanding.

4. Net change reflects any gain or loss from the preceding day. If you want to buy WorldWide Fund, you would pay $41.92 per share. WorldWide Fund increased in value twenty-two cents from the preceding day, or from $41.70 to $41.92. Mercury increased in value twenty-one cents from the preceding day, or from $19.62 to $19.83.

5. Total return for the year (January through September) is measured in a percent. WorldWide Fund has increased 11 percent; Mercury has performed better, with an increase of 20.2 percent.

REDUCING THE LOAD

Mutual funds can also be distinguished as "load" or "no-load" funds. A *load fund* is one in which a commission is charged that varies with the money invested: as much as 5 percent for the first $10,000, with a declining percentage commission when more money is invested. In load funds, commissions are taken out of your initial investment. If you invest $10,000, your actual starting investment will be $9,500 ($10,000 × 5 percent = $500; $10,000 − $500 = $9,500).

Because a fund charges a commission does not mean it is bad. There
are many closed-end load funds that have achieved impressive
results. Closed, open, load, no-load. . . . They all mean you have to
do your homework.

If you are being sold a load fund, don't be shy. Ask how much
commission you are paying. Does it make sense to purchase a load
fund? Sometimes. If you feel you need help in selecting funds and
putting together a game plan, it may well be worth it. The issue is
to know what you are paying for with any investment service.

Be wary of brokers who urge you to take one large sum and divide it
among two, three, or more different load funds. That's a highly unethical
way of making a large commission. A broker makes more money from
three 5-percent commissions on $10,000 ($1,500!) than from a reduced
commission rate for a single $30,000 transaction.

Obviously, if you buy into a load fund, you should plan to keep
your money invested for a fairly long term. The commission charged
on each transaction discourages investors from hopping from one fund
to the next. Anyone who invests in mutual funds should invest in a
family of funds; each has a different portfolio, each with a different
objective.

If you should decide you'd like to move your money from a growth-
oriented fund to an income-producing fund, you could do so with
minimal costs, if any, even over the phone. You might think a *no-load
fund* would be most advantageous because there are no commissions
paid to brokers. But you must keep in mind that no matter whether
you choose a load or a no-load fund, there will be a management fee
of some sort. These annual management fees should total about 1 percent of the fund assets for stock funds and less for bond and money
market funds.

Some funds don't charge an up-front commission. Instead, they charge
only when funds are sold, a *rear-end load.* The charges are usually expressed
as a percentage of your account value—which could be quite a bit if it has
appreciated. These funds are also known as 12(b)1 funds, named after a government rule that lets funds charge each shareholder up to 1 percent of
assets (effective July 1993) every year for advertising, mailing, and other
marketing expenses. Avoid them.

Avoid funds that charge a commission when you
reinvest your fund dividends, gains, or income.

Every mutual fund will give you a *prospectus,* a little booklet that describes the fund's investment objectives, costs, current investments, and management. To receive a prospectus call the fund's toll-free telephone number or, in the case of a load fund, ask the sales representative. No mutual fund sales may be made without the buyer having seen a prospectus. One of the *big* advantages of no-loads is that all of your money starts working for you right away.

Mutual fund companies must own printing presses—when you sign on, you
get a pen pal for life! Do read the newsletters that they send out.

The strategies suggested in this book are designed to enable you to make investment decisions on your own. In the case of mutual funds, I encourage you to choose a no-load fund. There are no commissions to pay and no brokers calling you, trying to sell you more. If you are doing the work, why pay someone a commission? Does this mean that there aren't any great performing load funds? No, of course there are. But, if you are truly asking a broker or financial planner to do all the legwork and research, expect to compensate them.

SPECIALIZED INVESTING

Mutual funds offer the advantage of many specialized funds. More and more investors are looking for opportunities that are not only financially sound but that also meet their own needs, temperaments, and ideals. It is one investment area where you can exercise some ethical or moral control. If it's important to consider social needs, here is a place. If you feel supportive of the military, for instance, you can choose a defense-oriented fund. If you resent the perceived elitism or arbitrary bureaucracy of companies such as IBM, you can select a fund that invests only in small companies.

A sector fund invests in a single industry, such as health care, transportation, or financial services. There are gold-oriented funds or science and technology funds. Global funds invest in both foreign and U.S. companies; international funds invest entirely in foreign securities; single-country funds focus on the securities of one country. Mutual funds, in other words, come in all shapes, sizes, and colors—something for everyone.

TOO MUCH FOR SO MANY

Many experts feel that mutual funds are too prolific and have thus created confusion. Indeed, thousands of funds beckon your investment dollars—there are more funds than there are companies on the New York Stock Exchange. Not only are there more, there is a lot of market hype and gimmickry involved in the increasingly competitive promotion of each one. However, with a little research the determined investor can find the funds that are right for her.

> Whether you are a seasoned investor or just beginning, choose a fund management company that has a variety of funds and allows you to switch among the family members.

GUIDEPOSTS FOR CHOOSING

There are several significant guideposts that will help in choosing a mutual fund. Ultimately, results are the final test—the measurement that might make you forgive all the confusion, hype, and high fees. Fund performance must at least keep up with inflation. Consider the average return figure over the last five years, keeping in mind that in investment circles it is traditionally believed the top performing fund of the year rarely repeats its performance the next year.

Give your mutual funds a midyear review. Compare their January-to-June returns with those of a Standard & Poor's 500 index (S&P)—the market average. Call the S&P Index Products hot line at 212-208-8855. If your fund is more than four percentage points lower than the average, consider switching funds.

Many of the large family funds (Fidelity, Janus, T. Rowe Price, Vanguard, Dreyfus, etc.) offer help in determining which of their funds you should invest in. T. Rowe Price has an "asset mix worksheet" that helps you decide how to allocate your moneys; Fidelity has a "fund match" program that helps you analyze your risk tolerance plus other variables. Ask.

Throughout the 1990s, several thousand new mutual funds were launched. Many of the new "kids" did not outperform the old-timers.

Nearly 60 percent of the start-ups underperformed the old-timers. One out of five lost money or returned less than 5 percent. During the same period of time, the S&P 500 index was up 10 percent.

The moral—if they don't have a track record . . . pass.

CONVENIENCE INVESTING

Most mutual fund families offer plans that allow you to make automatic monthly investments into your fund accounts. When you're choosing a no-load mutual fund, read the prospectus and application form to see if you can sign up for a program that will authorize the mutual fund company to *automatically withdraw* a certain amount of money from your personal checking account, or even from your company paycheck, to be invested in your mutual fund. Both my husband and I do this every month. It seems easier when it's automatic—part of our tithing to ourselves.

These automatic investment plans are the perfect way to fund an IRA or college savings program for a child. Plus, you're using the strategy of dollar cost averaging (DCA).

FOLLOW THE MAP

The prospectus of a mutual fund can be your guidepost—so do read it. It will state what the fund's objectives are, as well as give a breakdown of what it has invested in. Use it as a road map. It's not exciting reading—it's more like a cure for insomnia—but it does tell you who they are, how they have done, how much money is under management, and sometimes what kind of skeletons are lurking out there. Even though a prospectus is published only every thirteen months and will not give you a totally accurate fix on where the moneys are at any given time, it will offer valuable insights for your investment strategy.

PRIMARY FUND CATEGORIES

There are no strict rules on how funds are labeled. Let's look at the major categories next.

Aggressive Growth

These funds can make you a minifortune or zap you. Why? They invest in newer stocks of companies that have smaller capitalizations. Their goal is to seed maximum gains. You will never have heard of many of the companies they invest in. They also use investment techniques that carry greater risks.

Growth

The biggest group, growth funds typically buy shares of more established companies as they seek to achieve long-term capital appreciation. Many pay dividends, but the yield is minimal.

Growth and Income

Such funds invest in stocks with a dividend kicker on top of appreciation potential. These funds look for long-term growth and buy companies that have a track record spanning many years.

Income

The main appeal of income funds is high dividends, which often come from holding utility stocks or preferred shares of companies.

Bond

Corporate, U.S. government, and tax-free municipal bond funds are among the subcategories. Junk bond funds, which invest in low-rated but high-yield debt securities, are a current favorite because they continue to command double-digit interest returns. However, there is a big "but" here: junk means risk, sometimes excessive risk. Look carefully before you leap.

Specialty Funds

The newest kids on the block fall into this category. Anything you can imagine—health, energy, computer, communication, precious metals, international companies, money, even commodities are among your choices. A health-oriented fund will buy stocks only in the health-care and related industries. Some funds will be growth-oriented, others will seek income, and others combined in their objectives. There is truly something for everyone in this category.

DISCOUNT BROKERAGE FIRMS

You can purchase many no-load mutual funds through discount stock brokerage companies. The names and numbers of the largest of these brokerage firms are listed below. They do business through offices around the country and through telephone transactions.

Charles Schwab
800-648-5300
www.schwab.com

Fidelity Discount Brokerage Services
800-544-8666
www.fidelity.com

Quick & Reilly
800-926-0600
www.quick-reilly.com

Discover Brokerage Direct
800-688-6896
www.discoverbrokerage.com

Muriel Siebert & Co., Inc.
800-872-0444
www.siebertnet.com

If you are on AOL (America Online), you can go to its personal-finance Web site, which will then link you to just about anywhere you would think of going. Its address is *www.personalfinance.com.* This address can link you with any of the brokerage addresses listed plus others.

Discount brokerage firms offer you opportunities to buy and sell hundreds of no-load mutual funds. In most instances you are charged a small fee. The competition for this business is so great that fees are being reduced all the time. At most discount firms the fee is expressed as a percentage of the dollar amount being invested. Expect to pay about 0.6 percent, or a minimum of $30 per transaction.

Customers of Charles Schwab may buy and sell more than 100 of the most popular no-load mutual funds with no fee. The fund companies that have agreed to participate in this program are underwriting the cost in order to get wider distribution of their mutual funds. Expect other discounters to offer the same so they can keep up with Schwab.

Many investors find it worthwhile to pay small fees to buy no-load mutual funds because when you buy a variety of funds through a brokerage firm, you receive just one monthly statement detailing all of your mutual accounts. Also, if you want to buy and sell funds from different fund families, you don't have to wait until you receive a check from the sale of one fund in order to send in a purchase application to another fund. The brokerage firm will handle both transactions for you simultaneously.

SIMPLE RESOURCES REDUCE CONFUSION

Two other useful sources are available on your newsstand or by subscription.

SmartMoney magazine is a monthly publication that's a must for any woman interested in having her money grow. In the fall, it publishes its annual review of all the funds, ranking them, commenting on their strengths and weaknesses of management, and comparing previous years' performances. The best part? It's written in understandable English!

Forbes magazine, a biweekly publication, issues a special fund edition. *Forbes* is a real asset for the mutual fund investor. It does much the same as *SmartMoney* magazine, but it includes another ingredient: it ranks the fund's performance in a good and in a bad stock market. If it's an "A" it's terrific, but an "F" means avoid it like the plague.

I prefer to go with a fund that is rated "A" or better in a bad market and "B" or better in a good market. Why? Almost anyone can make money when the market is great, but the real pros shine when things aren't so hot. With this method, you eliminate almost 85 percent of the funds. Given all the choices you have, you need a starting point—this is a good one.

There are other magazines to definitely consider reading, including *Worth* and special financial issues from *U.S. News & World Report, Time,* and *Newsweek.* One of the very best of all the financial columnists today is *Newsweek*'s Jane Bryant Quinn. Her latest book, *Making the Most of Your Money* (Simon & Schuster 1997), belongs in your personal library as the ultimate in money references. Most likely your local newspaper presents excellent annual updates on the investment scene.

WHEN "AVERAGE" PUTS YOU AHEAD

Dollar cost averaging (DCA) is the process of making a regular investment in a stock or mutual fund of a fixed amount of money at a specific or regular time. I've chosen to include the what and how of DCA in the section on mutual funds (rather than on stocks) because you are more likely to put the practice into action with funds.

When you buy mutual funds, it is common to add money to the fund as long as you own it. You do it by reinvesting gains and dividends as well as by adding additional moneys. When you buy stocks, unless a dividend reinvestment plan is available, it is more common to own only the original shares purchased, not purchasing more of that stock to add to your holdings.

Successful investors practice the art of DCA. Let's say you invest $100 in your favorite fund on the tenth of each month. Today the cost is $15 per share. Last month it was $14.50 and the month before, $13. By averaging the three prices, your actual cost is $14.17 per share ($15 + 14.50 + 13 = $42.50; $42.50 ÷ 3 = $14.17): not the lowest price—but never the highest either.

> It is never too late to start DCA—even though the stock market may appear to be high. It's a guaranteed method of never paying top dollar for any stock or fund.

When the stock market, or the mutual fund you are investing in, is performing well, your $100 will buy fewer shares of the fund. If the market declines, your $100 monthly investment will automatically purchase more shares. Mutual fund shares are sold in thousandths of a share, so you don't have to worry about purchasing a full share when you invest; every dollar goes to work for you. It's a little more expensive to use DCA to buy individual stocks, since you may pay higher commissions to buy an odd number of shares.

Dollar cost averaging does not guarantee against loss. If the overall trend of the market is down, then you still would wind up with a loss for that period of time. That's why you should plan a program of dollar cost averaging to last at least several years. Success requires sticking to the plan in spite of market fluctuations.

Let's look at one of the funds from the Janus family, the Janus Fund, over a twenty-year period. If you had invested $100 each month, your total out-of-pocket commitment would be $24,000 ($100 × 12 × 20). In addition, all dividends and capital gains would have been reinvested. How would you have done? Quite well, to say the least. With your outlay over the years of $24,000, your investment would have increased in value from January 1, 1978 to $217,320.84 on December 31, 1998.

What will the next ten years show? Who knows, but with the fund's solid track record, investors should do well. Overall, this Janus family fund has continued to perform well for its shareholders. Are there other funds that have done as well as it has or better? You bet. When I first learned about mutual funds, there were about 400 to choose from. Now there are thousands. Some have done incredibly well, others not so well. Families of funds that have continued to outperform the market averages include Vanguard, Twentieth Century, T. Rowe Price, and the granddaddy of them all, Fidelity. You get to do the shopping. . . .

Hypothetical Investment in Janus Fund

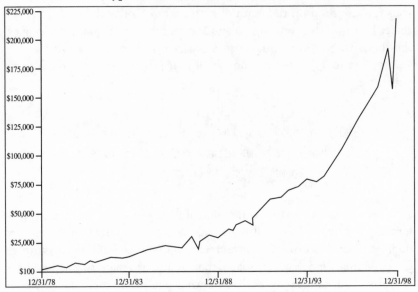

Data and artwork provided by Janus (3/99)

A hypothetical investment of $100 made every month for twenty years in Janus Fund starting on January 1, 1978, would be worth $217,321 on December 31, 1998, including reinvesting dividends and capital gains.

THE DOWNSIDE OF AVERAGING DOWN

Averaging down is the process of purchasing more of your investment as prices decline. Dollar cost averaging should not be confused with the concept of *averaging down*. Generally speaking, averaging down is used to rationalize the purchase of more of a losing investment. You then rationalize that the overall average cost of the total investment will then be lower. Wrong! It's completely different from dollar cost averaging—the strategy moves you in only one direction. You can average yourself into a deep hole by averaging down.

> When investments decline, you must reassess your original reason for purchasing.

When I was a stockbroker, I saw stocks decline in value. Some owners of these stocks would buy more. Here's how it works: someone buys 500 shares of a $10 stock for a $5,000 investment. The stock declines to $5 a share. Another 500 shares are purchased for $2,500. The total investment is $7,500, with an average cost of $7.50 per share.

Why should $7.50 seem so great as a purchase price? It isn't. The stock is still below your average purchase price and must exceed 7-1/2 for you to break even. Averaging down is usually a rationalization on your part for making an error—a wrong investment decision. There are, of course, always exceptions. Sometimes a stock can decline because of fear, even panic. Think about the huge swings in the stock market in 1998—up 150 points one day, down 300 the next, up the following. So, if you average down, it should really be because you believe the company is solid and will appreciate again.

THE TEN COMMANDMENTS OF MUTUAL FUND INVESTING

Success requires a plan—*your* money plan. Now that you have the basics, use these ten rules as a guide in your quest to evaluate the many options you have to choose from:

1. Know what your goal is. By doing your homework, you will discover which funds match those goals. You are always after the best return. Use a *no-load fund*. Historically, load funds have not outperformed no-load funds. If you selected a load fund instead, a heavy penalty is paid if you withdraw soon after purchase because you have already paid the commission up front. Also, check if there is a back-end fee.

2. Don't pick a small fund group. Select a family in the 100 to 300 million dollar range. They can afford to hire the best managers.

3. Avoid disaster. If your fund was alive in the 1970s, review its performance in the 1973–1974 and 1981–1982 periods when most funds did miserably. See how yours did in comparison to the pack. Look at the fourth-quarter results for 1987 and the third quarter for 1990. Both periods were humbling for most funds. That means you would have lost money. The 1990s have been extraordinary growth years for investors and funds

alike. The market will not always have the upward thrust it has enjoyed this past decade. Learn how much risk—emotional and financial—you are willing to take.

4. Avoid last year's top performer. Murphy's Law says it won't be number one this year.

5. Avoid a fund that has a peak and valley record. As long as it stays ahead of the averages, you will win. Sudden lurches lead to queasy stomachs, which lead to emotional bailouts, often at the wrong times. Patience is a virtue—be realistic with your "time horizons" for reaching your goals.

6. Determine if there has been a change in management or philosophy that might damage future performances. Fund companies are bought because they have done so well. The new team may not have the Midas touch. When Peter Lynch left Fidelity's Magellan Fund, it took several years before the fund got back on track.

7. Be wary of brand new funds. Why risk an unknown? If you are anxious to try something new, consider a fund whose manager has achieved a respected reputation elsewhere. Be wary of clone funds, as in the "Lookalike Fund" and the "Lookalike Fund 2." Rarely is the portfolio manager the same.

8. Reinvest all gains and dividends. Always.

9. Commit to regular investing over a period of time—dollar cost averaging.

10. If in doubt, spread your risk among several funds, but not all funds of the same type. If you are in the "World Fund" with one manager, don't buy a world-type fund with another.

Mutual funds are not the ultimate answer, nor the cure-all solution to your investment needs, but they should be an ingredient in your financial plan. Your age, tax status, investment philosophy, and personal philosophy will all influence your final decision. If you are realistic in your expectations (you are not going to double your money in a year), you understand that some years will be better than others—sounds like life. If you occasionally reassess your situation and goals, you will succeed in your financial game plan.

SUMMING UP—WHICH IS FOR YOU?

By now, you should realize there can be value, excitement, and choice in the stock market. You can go far toward matching your personality and interest with solid investment goals. But you can also go too far. The market has always risen and dropped—gone higher and dipped again. If you can get information to satisfy your questions and find an investment vehicle that matches your goals, the investment may be the right one for you. On the other hand, if there are gaps or holes in the information, be wise and pass, pass, pass.

The market does offer exciting opportunities, but before you invest your funds, understand the risks involved. Before diving in, determine several factors. Ask what the stock has done in the past. Is the present market "climate" conducive to overall investing? What do the stock market analysts project? And, finally, do you know anything about the product the company makes?

---

10 SMART MONEY MOVES TO DO BEFORE AND DURING INVESTING

1. **Become more observant.** When you go shopping, are there products and items that are always in short supply or out of stock? Ask the store's buyer why.

2. **Find out if the manufacturer of the product has publicly traded stock.** If the buyer tells you that the store can't keep the item in stock, the demand exceeds the supply of it. Who makes the product? Call a stockbroker and ask him or her to send you information about the company, or go to the library and see if there is a *Value Line* report on it. For your Smart Money strategy, this is good exercise in tracking down a company.

3. **Identify three items in your household that you replace every time you use them up.** Determine who makes each and see if there is a *Value Line* report on each company. If there is, what are the projections for the stock?

4. **Go to the Internet.** Type in *www.schwab.com.* Spend twenty to thirty minutes "surfing" the site.

5. **Subscribe to *SmartMoney* magazine.** It's one of the best, simplest to understand resources today.

6. **Contact the National Association of Investors Corporation at 248-583-6242.** Ask them to send you information on how to start an investment club.

7. **Identify a company that is well-known (e.g., Disney, McDonald's, Sears) and whose products you are familiar with.** Track down all the information you can get, including annual reports and recommendations made by brokerage firms. The *Value Line* will be helpful here.

8. **Start a mythical portfolio. Seed it with $100,000 of make-believe money.** "Buy" from five to ten stocks or mutual funds. Track their performance for the next year. If you think things don't look as promising as when you selected the investment, "sell" and buy something else. Record why so that you can review your own performance at year's end.

9. **Attend a lecture sponsored by a local brokerage or investment firm.**
   Your goal is to learn something about whatever the group is touting, not to sign on as a client—at least, not yet.

10. **Call a local brokerage or financial planning company.**
    Ask a representative to send you an informational packet about the firm and any copies of current research recommendations.

7

Become the Expert

Here's the BIG secret—good money sense is primarily a matter of trusting yourself and realizing your own potential for money management. Women are involved in elementary money management every day. Most of us are unaware of our positions as money managers because we don't speak the same jargon as the economists who work in government and the ivory towers of the financial community.

Women are quite good managers of money. The great majority handle the day-to-day family finances. And though they may not know the economic theories behind their financial maneuvers, when the tasks they perform instinctively are placed in the proper context—which is one of the aims of this book—money management begins to make sense.

> Smart Money Sense begins with believing in yourself, in understanding that you, as a woman, have a unique ability to turn possibilities into realities. Smart Money Sense is not packaged in some masculine learned logic. It begins with your own intuitive insights.

One of the differences between men and women in their investing styles is that men are more likely to jump on a "hot tip." Women don't; they wait to gather more information before they invest. Most believe that the "experts" are best at advising what to place your moneys in; this is a myth.

With just a few minutes each day, you, the Smart Money Woman you are, can acquire techniques to recognize what interest rates are doing, which industries are or aren't performing well, which companies are selling at a value price and which are overpriced, and how to spot a potential winner for your investment dollars.

INTUITION LEADS TO INVOLVEMENT

Smart Money Sense includes large doses of intuition and common sense. But even intuition needs information to be good, and that comes from involvement. One kind of involvement is simply awareness—paying attention to what goes on around you.

> Common sense is not so common. Trust yours.

Women traditionally have learned to be experts at shopping and finding bargains. Many families wouldn't eat without a woman's keen sense of timing and use of sales. They can apply the same skills that help them choose the best goods in a supermarket to the stock exchange and other markets.

PASS THE COFFEE

When I was a stockbroker, three of my colleagues and I observed that the price of coffee was getting very expensive, at least in coffee terms—a cup had gone from ten cents to twenty cents. We knew nothing that millions of other women shoppers didn't know. But instead of just knowing it, we noticed it. And we decided that increased prices meant coffee was becoming more valuable. My friends and I pooled our resources, bought a coffee contract on the commodities market, and made more than $70,000 profit within eight months.

Now, you may be thinking, "Is this what the media revealed Hillary Rodham Clinton did with cattle in 1994?" Not quite, although there were some similarities.

First, you must know that there are two types of players in commodities: hedgers and speculators. Hedgers are usually farmers or representatives of groups or companies that sell their product—corn, hogs, gold, wheat, wood, oil, orange juice, coffee, or whatever—to the marketplace. Hedgers can also be buyers of commodity contracts. Whether buyers or sellers, their intent is either to protect the price at which they have to buy (or sell) or to protect their obligation to the marketplace.

For example, coffee farmer Valdez from Brazil has agreed to deliver and sell 3,750,000 pounds of coffee to American buyers next fall. One contract of coffee is 37,500 green coffee bean pounds. So, farmer Valdez's objective is to harvest and sell 100 contracts (3,750,000 ÷ 37,500 = 100) to America at a specific price.

So far, so good. To protect himself from a crop disaster (coffee trees do get bugs and there are freezes in Brazil), farmer Valdez hedges himself. He buys 100 contracts in the commodities market. In other words, he "locks" in a price, which, no matter what happens to his trees, he can guarantee to meet his contract. Even if his trees die, he has a commitment from whomever sold him the contracts that they will deliver coffee to him— Valdez in turn can deliver to America. His strategy is like buying insurance.

Because of the shortage of coffee (or the perceived shortage) due to tree pest bugs and weather, global coffee prices change. This is exactly what the speculator wants. Speculators could care less about delivering or receiving thousands of pounds of coffee beans. In fact, that's the last thing they would want. They just want action—prices up or prices down.

In commodities, you can participate by putting all the money up for the entire amount of the contract or only about 10 percent of the contract value. In our case, the total contract's value was $50,250. We determined this by taking the price of coffee at that time (this was fall 1976), $1.34 a green coffee bean pound, and multiplying it by 37,500—the number of pounds in one contract. The commodity exchange required us to put up $5,000 to speculate.

Every time coffee changed a penny in price, the value of our contract was affected. Each penny movement equaled $375. If coffee increased four cents, the value of our contract increased $1,500; if coffee declined two cents, the value of our contract declined $750. How? An increase of four cents would mean that coffee is now $1.38 versus $1.34. Multiply $1.38 times 37,500 pounds and the result is $51,750. Subtract $50,250, and the difference is a $1,500 increase in value. Exciting, but it could go in reverse as well.

Our involvement in the evolving financial world made us aware of an opportunity. Our intuition and confidence made us act on it. Awareness of the marketplace and involvement in what was going on in the world were the keys to success. We celebrated when we made so much money, never imagining that we could make so much with our $5,000 investment. We were, however, *totally aware that we could also have lost everything*—all of our $5,000—if coffee declined in value.

Periodically, coffee makes headlines. In the mid-1990s coffee was in the news. Brazil had just experienced a killer frost. At that time Brazil supplied 30 percent of the world's coffee beans, and producers there estimated that the production from their trees would be down at least 30 percent over the next twelve months. Coffee commodities—or futures—soared in prices. Speculators saw the value of their contracts double within a week.

I can only guess the number of individuals who tried to make a quick buck with their life savings and found that what goes up also comes down. Once more, only hedgers—farmers, sellers, and buyers of product—or speculators—the folks with "kiss-off" money—should attempt to invest in such a situation. Unfortunately, news such as a rapid rise in prices tends to lure men and women. Whether the intent is to make a quick dollar or to make up for not planning, the results are usually the same for the novice: financial disaster.

Are there other disasters in these types of markets? Sure. If you are savvy and quick, you can take advantage of the misfortunes that Mother Nature delivers every once in a while. In the fall of 1998 Hurricane Mitch wiped out 90 percent of the banana crop. Now, you can't buy commodity futures in bananas, but you can buy or sell stock in bananas. Because Chiquita Banana would not have the product it had planned to sell, revenues would be reduced. So you would want to avoid owning the stock.

The commodity market is definitely not for everyone. As I get older, this kind of risk becomes totally inappropriate. High risk and speculation no longer fit my situation. Granted, I'm no longer financially responsible for my children. I am, though, responsible for adding to the retirement nest egg. I firmly believe that you must plan on being self-sufficient. Relying on governmental programs—even Social Security—as a sole support is foolish.

THE MIGHTY MORPHINS

Another example of this kind of awareness involves a company named Ban Dai America. My grandson Frankie discovered a TV show in the summer of 1993. So did millions of other kids. The show was *Mighty Morphin Power Rangers*. As Christmas approached, that's all Frankie talked about. His mom and I visited Toys 'R' Us. There was *no* merchandise. What a disappointment. Then I started to ask questions. I learned the reason why there was none: the average shelf life of any Power Ranger toy was seven hours! In investment jargon, that means that the demand was swamping the supply. There just weren't enough toys available for the buying public.

As 1994 rolled out, it became the number one show among both boys and girls. Throughout that year, there was a sign posted in Toys 'R' Us. An apology was posted from Ban Dai, saying the company regretted not being able to meet the enormous demand for its Power Ranger line. Articles routinely appeared in the *Wall Street Journal, USA Today*; it even made the cover story in *TV Guide*.

Frankie was thrilled to read about the upcoming new bad and good monsters—he and millions of other kids. An incredible ongoing demand built. One parent, who owned a car dealership, offered the manager of a local toy store a new car. The deal was that he would get one each of any Mighty Morphin Power Ranger toy that came into his store.

If you were to buy into a rapidly moving stock such as Ban Dai, you would also need to determine when to sell. As soon as you found that shelves were full of Power Rangers, which would indicate that the demand had diminished (i.e., shelf life is now a month), you would know that it's time to sell! Supply and Demand 101.

Morphin mania was so widespread that when I told Frankie that I was going to use the Morphins in an example in my talks, he told all his friends at school! He thought his grandma was very cool! Of course, Frankie is now a few years older. Mighty Morphin Power Rangers are no longer cool, at least for his age—he is now firmly entrenched in outer space.

Look at what happened in 1998 when Viagra became available. From being on the cover of *Newsweek* magazine to being the topic of every major news show and of jokes on the *Tonight Show*, Viagra was big news. Its manufacturer, Pfizer Inc., was also big news. In January 1998, the stock sold for $70 a share. When the demand for Viagra was reported, it skyrocketed to $120 a share, a 50 percent increase within six months. Not bad. So, how can you tap into what the obvious is? Start looking around.

What else is hot? How about filmmaker and producer George Lucas! The two-and-a-half minute trailer for the new *Star Wars* movie debuting in 1999 is the rage across America in December of 1998. I will bet my entire shoe collection that the distributor of *Star Wars, Episode 1,* will see a substantial increase in the value of its publicly traded stock shortly after the sequel is officially released in May 1999.

OUTSIDER'S INFORMATION

Do you use cosmetics? Are you getting older? If you answered yes to either of these two questions, there are a myriad of investment opportunities at your fingertips. According to Mary Kay Ash, founder of Mary Kay Cosmetics, we women spend on average $1,500 a year in cosmetics and sundries to make us look and feel good. What products sell the best? Who makes them?

The next time you're in a drugstore, beauty salon, or the cosmetics department at your favorite department store, ask what brands are selling and why. The odds are that the responses you get would be the same throughout the country. If you're from California, you soon learn (if you didn't already know) that many trends begin in the Golden State. Trends also begin on the East Coast.

One of the best newspapers in California is the *Los Angeles Times*. It's available at many newsstands and airports around the country. Do yourself a favor and pick up a Sunday edition once in a while. Or get a *Chicago Tribune* or the *New York Times*. Note the ads and articles in the *women's* and *living* sections. Big money is spent here, but you don't have to pay for the promotions: just buy the paper—a few dollars.

> If you'll commit to reading, often just scanning the newspapers every day, a wealth of information will come your way. Repeated headlines may mean investment potential or opportunity.

Do you wonder what to do with your cash—how to get the best yield or return without increasing your risk? Simply read the newspaper—the two- or three-paragraph article (usually on Tuesday) that tells you whether six-month treasury bill yields are up or down. If the yield goes up four weeks in a row, then move your funds to a money market fund or a ninety-day T-bill. Four weeks of increased rates is my signal that interest rates will continue to increase. In this position your funds will continue to reinvest at the higher rates.

On the other hand, if the Treasury yield decreases four weeks in a row, move to a one-year T-bill or one of the longer-term money market funds. Moving your money to these areas allows you to enjoy a higher interest rate than the funds that mature sooner. If interest rates are up one week and down the next or in any combination within a four-week period, stay put. No real change is developing.

To participate in treasury bills you need a minimum of $1,000. If that is beyond your means, then there are many money market funds that will invest your money. In fact, some of the funds invest only in treasury obligations, yet have a minimum buy in of only a few hundred dollars. There is always something for everyone. Just ask.

Is what I'm sharing inside information? Absolutely not—it's information that is available through newspapers and magazines and on radio and television. It is information that is available to anyone—including you.

THE REAL INSIDE SCOOP:
IDENTIFYING YOUR SOURCES

Involvement and identification go hand in hand. Involvement also means keeping informed. This does not mean taking crash courses in securities law, Fannie Mae's, or CPI implications. Nor does it mean reading the stock market report each day to check the status of 100 shares of your favorite stock.

It does mean reading the newspapers. It means a commitment of fifteen to twenty minutes a day to read the front page of your local paper, as well as the headlines and the first three or four paragraphs of each story in the business section. After a while you will recognize that reports of large layoffs within a particular industry or field of business indicate a fall within that field. Stay away from related investments.

Similarly, dividend drops or store or office closings indicate trouble. On the other hand, a series of new hirings or promotions and the engagement of a larger advertising firm all indicate business is on the move. After a while you will begin to read more analytically. Declining (or rising) interest rates, crop failures, devaluation of the dollar, and the toppling of governments may all seem irrelevant to you on a day-to-day basis, but they will affect your investments.

> It is not the daily stock market changes that will affect your stock. It is the underlying prevailing trends in population densities, housing and business preferences, tax advantages, and real estate values.

I've said you don't need much more than your daily newspaper to keep abreast of investment trends. Certainly it is unwise, even downright confusing, to get caught up in the myriad investment newsletters, advice columns, and broker "tips" that abound. But there are three sources outside of your local paper that can be helpful.

One is the *Wall Street Journal*, the eminent, authoritative, up-to-date, but very readable daily business newspaper. The second is the accessible, respectable, highly relevant *Value Line Investment Survey*, published by Value Line, Inc. and described in the sixth chapter.

A third source is general magazines such as *Newsweek*, *Time*, *Business Week*, and *U.S. News & World Report*, which all have articles on current trends, money, and the overall economy. Peruse a few of them just to get a feel for how various ideas are presented.

> Isn't your financial independence worth twenty minutes of your time each day?

When looking at the various financial opportunities at your disposal, it's important that you feel comfortable with the financial world. You must be able to identify relevant information that comes your way and recognize the trends that affect the money game. As you begin to probe investment options, especially with individual stocks, you will discover the world of annual reports.

IT's BETWEEN THE LINES— UNDERSTANDING ANNUAL REPORTS

I strongly believe that just about anything you need to know about a company or stock is at your fingertips or a phone call away. I call it "outside information," those newspapers, magazines, TV and radio programs, the local grapevine, associations—you name it. They all provide hints, leads, and information on who is doing what to whom in business.

Another excellent source, provided to any shareholder of stock, is also available to you for the asking. Any company that trades stock has an annual corporate report. These next guidelines will help you understand the information you come across in reading an annual report. If such a report seems intimidating, there are resources, in other words, that translate the data in such reports into easily digestible facts and figures.

WATCH THE UNDERDOGS!

Because of your experience with economic cycles, you should be able to recognize, evaluate, and even benefit from "undervalued" situations. Even companies that have gone through and survived bankruptcy can offer interesting investment opportunities. But only if management is able to turn the situation around and again succeed in the business environment. Such companies will be undervalued as they emerge from bankruptcy because the investing community has lost faith in them.

Use the *Value Line Investment Survey* referred to earlier. Look into companies that are having serious financial difficulty and are publicly traded. The annual reports and the latest interim reports will be of great assistance. Also check in the Standard & Poor's individual company reports or the corporate records that Standard & Poor's publishes. Your library carries copies in its reference section.

If you do not know where to obtain these reports, merely check with an intermediate-sized library or brokerage firm and request them. If you opt to go to the library, make copies of the reports that interest you, because usually you cannot check them out.

If you already have a broker, you should call him or her and ask for a copy of the latest report from both services. Like all annual reports, Standard & Poor's and *Value Line* carry not only the corporate office address of the firm you are interested in, but also identify the chief executive officers. With this information in hand, you can write or call the company and request a copy of their annual report.

CORPORATE REPORT CARDS

Annual reports are interesting instruments. The amount of money invested in glossy pictures and presentation is phenomenal. An annual report provides a lot of information, but to evaluate it you should learn where to concentrate your energies. First of all, you want to make sure the report conforms to generally accepted financial reporting practices. This means that a certified public accountant has verified the numbers, balanced them out, and stated that in his or her opinion, the company conforms.

If you don't see the words *generally accepted accounting principles* (GAAP) at the end of or on the back of the report, then you should be very cautious; that company is asking you to accept their figures on faith. An unbiased CPA has not been able to or been allowed to validate or verify the exactness of the financial information provided by the company.

Prior to studying the balance sheet (which indicates the net worth of the company) and the income statement (income and expenses are listed), look at the footnotes. Footnotes will tell you if the company has incurred any additional debt and at what cost and maturity level (long-term or short-term). It will also let you know whether they have had any accounting changes, as well as any once-in-a-lifetime (extraordinary) increases in revenues or write-offs. Sometimes accounting changes can be positive.

The company could change from FIFO accounting to LIFO accounting. This means that prior to the current year their inventory value was based on *first in, first out*, not on *last in, first out*. In LIFO accounting, the value of the inventory would be carried at the current inflated levels. This is actually a more conservative way to state the position of a company. LIFO accounting gives a truer picture of current market reaction. At the end of the fiscal year, the bottom line is brought about and does not show an extraordinary jump or gain in earnings.

In FIFO accounting the overall cost is reflected at a substantially lower value. The inventory costs reflect purchases of inventory several months or even years prior, before prices increased due to inflation. Their products are being moved off the shelf, and the margin between cost and selling price is greater. Thus, the company will show a greater percentage increase in earnings when the quarter or year finishes.

The problem with FIFO is that this method of accounting often produces a nonrecurring gain. A company that reports extraordinary gains usually employs FIFO accounting. The following year, however, they must replace the inventory at *current* market prices. Because of the higher replacement costs, they could actually show a decrease in profit. This decrease may be reflected negatively in the marketplace, and a decline in the company's stock price could be the result.

Sometimes a company restates its earnings by switching from one accounting method to another. This rattles the investment community. Sometimes it is viewed as positive, sometimes as negative. Beware of a company that switches to FIFO accounting after they have historically used LIFO. They may be trying to bolster a less-than-rosy financial picture. As a rule, if the company uses or switches to the LIFO method, it does have an overall calming effect on both stock analysts and investors.

Often companies sell divisions and subdivisions to other companies or individuals. If you have noticed a substantial increase in earnings per share, it makes sense to verify whether it is attributed to an actual increase in sales revenues (products they ordinarily sell) or to the sale of an asset or division of the company. If a company sells a major division, settles litigation, or even sells off some of its real estate, these revenues will be classified as *nonrecurring* gains, or revenues, or losses on the balance sheet.

Keep in mind that *nonrecurring* is exactly what it means—a one-time-only occurrence. When reviewing your stock or considering a purchase of stock in a company that reports revenues derived from nonrecurring entities, be cautious. They may report a substantial increase in sales or earnings per share over the prior year. But if you find, in probing into the balance sheet, that the revenue is due to a nonrecurring source, the earnings may not be increasing—and could, in fact, be decreasing. *Make sure to read between the lines.*

Frequently, when companies begin to sell divisions, they are experiencing major financial problems. The most salable of their divisions are, of course, their more profitable ones. If they do sell off the profitable segments, the remaining company could be a mere shell, or even be debt ridden, and the stock could quickly become valueless. This has happened, and the benefit always goes to the *original* major stockholders. In the long run, or even the short run, this could have a substantial negative effect on a company whose annual report you are reading.

If a company has sold additional shares to the general public or bought back shares on the open market, footnotes will also reflect that. They should, in fact, restate the total number of shares outstanding (available for sale) and whether there has been an increase or decrease in the number.

The report will contain a letter from the president, the chairman of the board, or both. He or she gives an update on what happened the preceding year as well as a projection of how the company is expected to fare during the coming year(s). If a company has had problems, the executive should say so in the letter and should also include information on what has been done to rectify them.

Hopefully, you are now preparing your own net worth statements on an annual basis. A company's net worth is reflected in its balance sheet. When examining the balance sheet, you will note that all its assets are laid out on the left side and are broken into areas such as *current* and *other* assets. On the right side of the page the liabilities are laid out. You will notice current liabilities and liabilities that are due a year or more after the company's year-end.

Most annual reports set forth not only the current status of a company, but also that of its preceding four years. This allows you to get a quick view of whether the current assets, such as cash, are increasing or decreasing. It shows the inventory position of the company. When you deduct current liabilities from current assets (assuming that the assets are greater than the liabilities) you get what is called the *net working capital. This is an essential figure to examine.*

Most healthy companies have what is known as a two-to-one ratio—for every dollar in current liabilities, there should be two dollars in current assets. If the company you are looking at carries inventory, subtract that figure from the current assets and then compare the result with current liability. This will give you what is called a *quick ratio*, and it should be one to one—for every dollar of liability, there should be one dollar of assets.

If you find the ratios are lower than those I have cited, there might be a problem. For example, if the company doesn't have the one-to-one ratio, it may not be able to meet any of the short-term debts that mature within the year, and it may have to reduce or eliminate a dividend that would normally have been paid.

Income from your investments becomes important when you retire and rely on dividends and interest. The last thing you then want is to be notified on the nightly news that your stock's dividend will be reduced or eliminated. Warning signs usually show up in the balance sheet. Watch for increases in liabilities, decreases in earnings, or both.

The *net worth* of a company is the *stockholders' equity*. Also referred to as "shareholder equity," it is simply the difference between total assets and total liabilities. If stockholders' equity in a company is $500,000 and there are 10,000 shares outstanding, you merely divide 10,000 into $500,000 to learn that each share would bring $50 upon liquidation. This is known as *book value*, and it has little to do with the company's current market trading value.

It is important for you to pay close attention to the liabilities side and in particular to increased amounts allocated to either short-term or long-term debts. If a company is growing aggressively and doing well, as a rule there are minimal problems in acquiring working capital and thus debt. Borrowing is often necessary because it helps fuel growth, which usually results in additional revenues and bottom-line profits. However, borrowing could spell disaster for a company that continues to incur debt to help underwrite its operating expenses during times of declining revenues.

Once a company is in a bankruptcy proceeding, which is also known as *Chapter 11* or *reorganization*, there may be a significant opportunity for a return to good health. But recovery occurs only if the various creditors work together, allow the company to continue operation, and allow the company to pull itself out of its troubles.

One other item that is always included in an annual report is the income and expense statement. Often you will hear or read that companies make so much per share. Their earnings are up, down, or flat. This is a good reason for looking at the footnotes. Earnings per share can be increased artificially if a company has, for whatever reason, sold a portion of its assets to bring in revenues.

To have a true picture of the actual sales of the company, it is important to deduct any nonrecurring revenues that are generated from one-time-only sales. On the other hand, if the company has sold a division that was actually a drain on other more profitable divisions, the profits may begin to increase significantly as a result of selling the weak division. Again, read the footnotes.

> In analyzing a company, I can't overstate the need to review the annual reports for the last few years. Equally important is a comparison study of what is going on in the particular industry segment.

You can do this by referring to the *Value Line Investment Survey*. It examines individual companies within industry groups and provides you with a barometric reading of how they all are doing, what kind of debts they are carrying, what kind of growth patterns they are showing, new product directions, and the range of stock prices during good times and bad.

The company that you are analyzing may be a true underdog and ready to take off. On the other hand, it could be at the height of its value and ready to plummet. Information from an annual report and supplemental reports such as the *Value Line Investment Survey* and Standard & Poor's sheets are essential aspects of decision making on stock market investments.

One final word here. Even though an annual report may indicate that a company is turning around, doing well, or comparing favorably with others in the industry, there is no guarantee that your stock will increase in value. If the economic environment is generally negative or if the company you are looking at is not enjoying a favorable press, it may make sense to step aside until things look better.

SUMMING UP—THE FOUR I'S ARE YOUR FRIENDS

In these days of money market funds and other instruments that offer liquidity with a comparable rate of return (such as CDs and U.S. Treasury securities), it is important to determine, prior to purchasing shares in a company, whether your expected return (via profits) or yield (via dividends) is comparable to the inflation rate. If you invest in the stock market, your objective should be to achieve a greater rate of return than money market funds would offer.

It is very important to note that, throughout this century, the stock market investment has won out over inflation. With your growing knowledge of Smart Money Moves and a little patience you, too, should be able to outperform the inflation rate.

Let the *Four I's* be the beginning of successful stewardship: intuition, involvement, information, and identification. Remember, they are only part of a process. Trusting your intuition, involving yourself with the marketplace, informing yourself on business news, and identifying investment trends all require commitment. Added to these four I's, patience and perseverance will yield the wisdom you need for a Smart Money Move.

One of my favorite phrases is that common sense is not so common! Use yours.

---

10 Smart Money Moves
to Create Expertise

1. **Make a list of all the cosmetics and sundry products that you use.** Now, determine what companies make them. Over the next three months, keep your eyes and ears peeled for any news, good or bad, about the product. Depending on what you hear, if you had money, would you buy stock in the company?

2. **You've just heard on the evening news that a breakthrough product has been approved by the FDA that will end heart disease in women. You didn't catch the name of the manufacturing company. What do you do?** Call the station and ask.

3. **You now know the name of the company. Does this sound like an investment opportunity?** Absolutely. According to the American Heart Association and the National Cancer Association, heart disease is the number one killer of all women (lung cancer is number two, and breast cancer number three).

4. **If you are in an investment club, offer to head up the research for the next meeting of several stocks your club is considering.** Hit the library and use the Internet—both will yield more than enough to share at your next meeting.

5. **Scan the newspapers, especially the business sections, for news—bad or good. If you had money to invest, what would some of your options be?** Think about buying stock,

selling it, avoiding stock, finding a merger or takeover partner, expansion possibilities, career opportunities, and so
forth.

6. **Think of a time when your intuition, your gut reaction,
   told you to do something.** Did you? What happened—was
   the outcome positive, negative, or neutral?

7. **Most women want security. What does an investment
   need to be to make you feel secure?** Only you can
   answer this one.

8. **Call three companies that are publicly traded and
   whose products you regularly use. Ask them to send
   you their annual reports.** Use the guidelines suggested in
   this chapter. Look for any hedged statements in the letter
   from the chairman or president and note any changes
   from the preceding year in the company's financial condi-
   tion.

9. **Ask a kid over the age of nine—yours, your niece or
   nephew, a grandchild, a friend's or the next-door
   neighbor's, what their friends are spending their
   money on.** Kids between the ages of nine and nineteen
   spend more than 100 billion dollars a year on stuff. Who
   makes the products they buy? Can you invest in the companies?

10. **Go down to a Toys 'R' Us, Costco, Sam's, Wal-Mart,
    Home Depot, Home Base, CompUSA, Sears, or JC
    Penney and wander into the department of your
    choice. Ask for the buyer of the department and sec-
    tion, and ask the individual which merchandise or
    product line is selling. Ask if she or he has an opinion
    as to why it's selling so well.** If you had any money to
    invest, would you? What would you do to learn more
    about any of the products or companies cited?

Use Borrowed Money Wisely

8

Too many people today are influenced by the microwave approach—get things now and be quick about it. Consumer debt, bankruptcies, and foreclosures are at an all-time high. Some women fear the use of any type of credit is bad news, from credit cards to mortgages to borrowing to adding needed cash capital for a growing business. You may be one of them.

Paying cash for items is an excellent practice to hone. There are times when borrowing makes Smart Money Sense. Few have enough cash today to buy a car or a home outright. There are times when certain retail sales occur that your borrowing for a purchase, even for just a month or two, makes sound financial advice.

Every time I do a radio show with a theme on money, the subject of credit—the problems with it—leads to listeners' questions. If there are twenty calls, almost half will be on this one topic alone. Credit is an integral part of a woman's life. So you will find just about everything you need to know about the consumer credit world in order to be a Smart Money Woman on the following pages—and that's a lot of information. Get out your highlighter and Post-its.

CREDIT: FRIEND AND FOE

Americans owe more money than do the people of any other Western civilization! We get deeper into debt every year. In 1996 Americans crossed the trillion-dollar mark with charges using credit. More than $400 billion is owed in credit card balances alone, with the average household carrying more than a $6,000 debt. Ouch!

The average rate paid on a credit card balance is 18 percent. As the 1990s ended, Americans carried a balance of some $400 billion on their cards— that's $72 billion *in interest.* For every $6,000 in debt (the national average), $1,080 is added for interest charges! Credit card companies are routinely slapping an extra $15 to $20 charge on your balance if you are even *one day* over the day due or you go *one dollar* over your preassigned limit. That could amount to a 100 percent plus interest charge! Ouch, ouch, and more ouch.

> Know what using plastic really costs. If your card carries a 19.8 percent rate and you buy a new TV for $500 and spread the payoff over a twenty-four-month period, you actually pay $637. The add-on interest increases your real cost by 27 percent!

You may be one of the few who really do pay off every credit card in full every month before the due date. Even if that's the case, do not skip this chapter. Why? Because errors are made. Not in your paying your bills. No, it's in the way creditors report your paying habits to the credit-reporting agencies.

There's a few trillion more dollars owed out there, including

- more than $250 billion in auto loans,
- mortgage debt exceeding $3 trillion,
- corporations with $3.6 trillion in debt reported on their books,
- state and local governments that owe in excess of $900 billion, and
- the National Debt, exceeding $4 trillion.

Looking at these numbers, no wonder so many people don't worry about a few thousand dollars they owe! But you should. Credit can be expensive. Certainly, creating unmanageable debt is foolish, even destructive. But using debt or credit as a tool in a long-term, cogent financial plan is smart. It is wise and sound financial management. It's a Smart Money Move.

Using your assets to your best advantage includes learning to take full advantage of the credit your net worth and earning power entitle you to. The rich may still rule the poor, but the borrower no longer needs to be slave to anyone, much less the lender.

Because of credit abuse, many feel that using credit is bad. Many believe that use of credit cards and even buying on any form of credit are taboo, even sinful. Too much credit is easily misused and can have devastating results. And many may find they have trouble controlling their spending when it's so easy to present that all-too-familiar card. But if credit is used properly, it can be your friend, not your foe.

> Credit takes on many different forms. It has applications and implications on both short- and long-term bases. Your Smart Money Move is to understand and use credit wisely.

CREDIT IS A FACT OF LIFE

Credit is an inescapable part of modern life. All of us at one time or another will have to acquire money from an outside source. You can use credit to improve your situation, provided you act wisely and make good use of another economic phenomenon—borrowing. If you ask most people what they use banks for, they would probably tell you for a checking or savings account. Both are items in which money is deposited with the bank. Have you ever thought what would happen if the bank were merely a depository? It would go out of business. In order for a bank to succeed, it must also lend money.

The age of yuppies parallels the days of the 1970s and early 1980s, days crazy with high inflation. A dramatic increase in consumer credit took place. Everyone had credit cards, some too many. They were the *in* thing to have. Bankers were openly soliciting unsecured loans to customers and potential new customers. This means they would loan money without having anything as collateral (such as a car, home, business, or savings account). Today home owners are told that they can borrow 125 percent of the value of their home, and mailboxes routinely are filled with new credit card solicitations. It feels like free money is everywhere!

THE RIGHT WAY

Learning to use credit properly is a step toward stewardship of your money. Credit can work to accelerate your net worth, balancing the effects of inflation. At the same time, it can also make your life easier and more comfortable, freeing and giving you more energy and more assets to devote to your priorities.

Few would deny the value of saving money. But have you ever considered how credit is like savings? Having credit available is similar to having savings in a bank. If you have established some credit rating by buying on time and paying off on time, if you have focused on building a proper relationship with the bank manager over the years and have demonstrated you are a good, responsible citizen with stable employment and the ability to repay, your bank would most likely be delighted to lend you $5,000 on an unsecured basis. Having that *ability* to borrow $5,000 has the same effect as having $5,000 in the bank. It's there in case you need it. It's there for the rainy day that won't quit.

That same reasoning applies to credit cards. What credit cards represent is the ability to obtain cash, goods, or services. They sometimes take the place of savings, if necessary. You likely know someone who has lost his or her job or had a sudden financial burden fall on them.

As the 1990s come to a close, birthing the new millennium, it's hard to look back at the beginning of the decade. In the "downsizing" era of the decade's first few years, many good families, both husband and wife, found themselves at the unemployment office. Businesses right and left cut back on staff. Families who had had comfortable incomes found living while unemployed next to impossible as they searched for new jobs. They had no cash to pay for ongoing living expenses until they turned themselves around.

Many people never know how badly off they are financially until it's nearly too late. Having credit cards that have been paid regularly and on time can act as that savings if such a disaster hits. It doesn't mean you rush out and run them up, buying extravagant presents or borrowing cash advances that carry an expensive interest cost. It means simply that you have it there for that rainy day if your savings are ever exhausted—*if all else fails.*

I write about this from personal experience. In the early 1980s I owned my own business in partnership with another woman. Part of our business was buying old buildings and restoring them. My partner took on another partner—one called drugs. Several hundred thousand dollars were missing from a construction loan that my signature was on. The bank demanded that I pay it. Eventually I did.

Over the next few years, a fire sale was done on all our assets. We lost our home, cars, all investments; all jewelry and art was sold. I even sold clothes to feed my three teenagers. Everything material built up over a ten-year period—gone! Over one million dollars in value.

The stress was unbelievable—my health was a mess, my marriage was in jeopardy, even the dog lost her hair! If I had not had a credit card, there were many times my family would not have eaten.

> I know that many of you have had situations where you became destitute because of an extraordinary event: a lost job, divorce, someone in debt to you who didn't pay back. Please realize you are not alone.

Eventually, in my case, the bank got back all their money. And they never even said, "Thank you." Ten years ago, my family assessed our situation. I felt strongly that California was just too expensive to live in. As a native, this was a painful admission. My husband did not want to move, my older daughter has a good job with Lockheed, and my other daughter worked for me. I had to sell them on it.

My eldest son had died in 1983, two years after the embezzlement. Just driving on the streets or across the bridge from which he had fallen gave me the willies. I wanted out—the sooner, the better. One of my personal goals was to own a home again. I had come to the conclusion that that was almost impossible in California.

As a speaker, I had the opportunity to visit many places. Two cities stood out: Seattle and Denver. After careful probing, I determined that Denver was the more suitable—the cost of living was lower, and its being based closer to the middle of the country was a definite advantage for travel purposes that related to my speaking business. Then I had to convince my family.

On Labor Day weekend, the plan was put into place. The previous June the department my husband was chairman of had been eliminated from the college where he taught. John had reluctantly gone to the unemployment office as he looked for work. Sheryl, my youngest daughter, had just come out of a painful divorce. She and my grandson, Frankie (three years old at the time), were ready for a change. It seemed that we had been hitting an overwhelming number of "potholes" during the past decade. Sheryl and John were willing to walk through the open window for a look-see. Frankie was thrilled to go anywhere, as long as he was with his family.

We flew to Colorado using airline award certificates from all my travel, stayed with a friend, and looked around. In Denver we found real estate values quite depressed, especially compared with California's. My dream of owning a home again might come true!

When doors close, windows may open. Sheryl found a home—imagine a twenty-four-year-old buying her own home with her own money! John and I found a lovely home the previous owner had tried to sell for more than a year. Both were acquired with negotiating and minimal dollars.

I knew that because we had credit set up, when disaster hit, we could meet our bare-essential needs. So pressure was taken off for a few months until our cash flow was going again. It took several years to get back on track.

WHAT SHOULD YOU HAVE?

Savings sometimes become the least best alternative. The best alternative, in my opinion, is having your money out there working and multiplying.

Credit cards can actually help build a strong arsenal and personal financial plan. Some cards can be obtained without a fee; others have annual charges. Five years ago it was common for people to have many credit cards in their wallets and purses. Today, that has changed. With many stores and vendors accepting credit cards other than their own, you don't need to carry or possess lots of cards.

It makes sense to have a Visa and MasterCard, as well as one of the business cards, such as American Express or Diners Club. Discover, Visa, and MasterCard impose limitations on how much can be charged. Business card companies don't have limitations, and usually don't assess interest as long as your bill is paid off in full within sixty days of its receipt.

If you travel, a business card is vital, especially for your airline tickets, hotel, and car rental costs. You *cannot* rent a car without a credit card, even if your intent is to pay cash. Major department stores take Visa, MasterCard, even American Express. Sears's Discover card is like a super MasterCard, acceptable at retailers other than Sears; it gives its holder the ability to withdraw cash at any Sears store, as well as at ATMs located throughout the United States. Many of the credit cards offer free airline miles and cash or credit back when you accumulate some amount of points (points being the equivalent of dollars charged).

Credit cards can also be used to keep track of different types of payments. You may have some expenses that are tax deductible or business related. Put those on your Visa card. Your personal expenses can be placed on your MasterCard or vice versa. The credit card companies send a detailed statement at the end of the billing period stating where you spent the money, including the establishment's name, such as a restaurant. It's a useful and detailed list of your transactions completed in any given month.

Know what the billing cycle of your card is. The dates are usually noted on your statement as the billing period. Charges and payments received after that date will be noted on the next month's statement. If you have to buy any major item, purchase it right after that date; it will give you a longer period before you have to pay the funds back. Your statement, which reflects the purchase, will not come until the following month. Normally you have several days after receiving the statement before payment is due. When bills state a specific date due, it is common to have a grace period, seven to fifteen days after the due date, to actually pay your bill before your payment is considered late.

With this strategy of buying right after the billing period, not paying until after you receive the next statement, and taking advantage of the grace period, you have gained from six to seven weeks of float time. Over a period of time, this credit can add up to a significant amount of money. It is far smarter than paying 18- to 20-plus percent on outstanding credit card balances. You stretch your budget farther and justify the annual credit card cost.

WARNING, WARNING, WARNING!

A word of caution is in order here: beware of the danger of running too many charges that cannot be paid off when your bill comes. To avoid any finance charges, your credit card statements must be paid in full before the due date. What you have done is used the issuing card company's money for a short period of time to purchase the goods or services you needed. This is called a *float*.

MAKING LOW-INTEREST RATES THE NORM

If you have outstanding credit card debt, you want to pay the lowest interest rate possible while you pay it off. One strategy is to get a lower credit card interest rate by applying for a new card. However, get your magnifying glass out. Some offers may be too good to be true. One bank offers a low 3.9 percent rate (sounds good if you pay over 20 percent). For example, after you transfer the old balance to it, any new purchases trigger a change—the entire balance will be increased to a much higher interest rate, such as 15.9 percent.

> If you are thinking, she's really on the "Lower the Interest" bandwagon—you're right. Why? Because less than 30 percent of the American public pays under 16 percent on their credit card balances.

Today's bank marketing strategies offer consumers low introductory bank card rates, encouraging customers to transfer existing balances from other institutions. Why? Because with credit card saturation of the current market (almost every qualifying adult has two cards), the name of the game is not to recruit new cardholders, but rather to have current cardholders play "musical cards."

Many banks are offering "teaser rates" to lure you in—that 3.9 percent special. You *must* read all the print and conditions in the contract. Before you jump ship, do what was suggested in Smart Money Move #4 on Tithing—call your present card company representative and remind him or her that your mailbox is brimming with rival offers—ask for a lower rate. This technique has worked to get annual fees waived and interest rates lowered. You can't get it if you don't ask for it.

If a credit card issuer balks at giving you a lower rate, shop around—carefully. A nonprofit consumer education group called Bankcard Holders of America publishes a monthly list of the low-rate cards, available for $4. You can contact them at 800-327-7300 or 703-481-1110. Many of the lowest-rate cards are from regional or smaller banks that do not send out mass solicitations—they can't afford to because their profit margins are much smaller than the banks that bombard you with hype.

There are three other sources to find the best credit card deals at your fingertips. Your newspaper carries a breakdown on a weekly basis of the best cards to use. Look for it in your Sunday newspaper. If you don't find it, call the business section of the paper and ask when it runs. *Money* magazine also carries it in each issue. Another great source is on your computer (or the library's). Go on-line and type in *www.money.com/rates.com*. Click on Best Rates—it will identify the lowest rates currently available on credit cards, mortgages, auto loans, and much more.

CREDIT'S UNWRITTEN RULES

Before credit gets out of control, there are lots of "unwritten rules" for its use. By identifying and following them, you will be in control and using credit wisely. Once you accomplish this feat, you'll find that many of the things that women want today—solvency, simplicity, solutions, sanity, satisfaction, safety, security, stability, strategy, and smarts will be bundled in the wise use of credit and using someone else's (i.e., the bank's) money.

> If you transfer your balance from one card to another, close the old card out immediately. The idea is not to expand your credit, but to reduce the cost. Avoid all cards with costly billing practices, in spite of their advertised lower rates.

Don't apply for more than one or two credit cards at a time. Each inquiry about your credit is included in your credit report. If too many credit grantors inquire at once, they may become suspicious of your intention.

Make it a personal rule not to charge "disposable" items, such as gasoline and food, on your credit card. These items are long gone by the time you receive your credit card bill. Unless you need the records for a business deduction, pay cash for food, restaurant meals, and gasoline.

One of the newest scams involves companies that promise to get you a low-interest-rate credit card—for a fee. Avoid these middle people. Contact the card issuer directly, using the lists available from Bankcard Holders of America at 800-327-7300. Do not pay a fee unless the card is actually issued to you, at which time the fee will be added to your account balance.

You may not have to change card issuers to get a lower rate finance charge. Most card issuers will lower your rate if you have a good payment record with them. Call the toll-free number on your bill and inform the issuer that you're planning to switch unless you get a lower rate, and then see if they'll offer you a better deal.

Here's what I found when a dozen of my friends called the issuers of their credit cards: nine out of ten were immediately offered lower rates on the phone. This is definitely worth your time. The one constant exception was the Discover card.

Apply for a secured credit card. If you don't have a credit history or have had problems in the past, this may be for you. You deposit funds into a savings type of account, earning interest, and your financial institution issues credit equal to your deposit. Warning—go straight to your bank or savings and loan. Do not use a "card shopping service" or other type of middleman. Bankcard Holders of America can offer you a complete list of institutions that offer secured cards.

Keep an updated list of all your cards. Make a list of *all* the credit cards (and other cards, such as insurance and driver's license) you keep in your purse or wallet. Note the account number, and next to it place the toll-free phone number that you have been given to call in case of loss or theft. (You'll find that number on your monthly bill.) Determine the due date and if there is a grace period for payment. And know your liability in the event that your cards are lost or stolen:

- If you report the loss of your credit cards *before* they are used, you have no liability for *any* charges.

- If you report the loss of your credit cards, and they have been used, you are liable for the first $50 charged on each card. Many creditors waive their right to charge you for the first $50.

- If a lost or stolen card is used for a mail-order purchase and is not presented directly to the merchant, you are not liable for any of the purchase.

There are registration services that offer to limit your entire liability on lost or stolen cards. It isn't free. The convenience is that you make only one phone call. The service in turn contacts all your creditors. Check your home owner or rental insurance policy to see if it covers the $50 deductible on each credit card.

Know your credit card rights. All merchants sign their own agreements with card issuers such as Visa, MasterCard, and American Express. These standard agreements include the following:

- Merchants may not ask for your phone number or driver's license in order to accept your card.

- Merchants should not ask for your credit card number as a basis to accept a check, and you should not allow your credit card number to be written on the back of your check. Also, merchants are not allowed to charge the cost of a bounced check to your credit card, even if they have your card number.

- Visa and MasterCard prohibit merchants from requiring a minimum dollar amount purchase in order to use your card. American Express has the same policy in most states. This doesn't mean that they don't do it—some merchants do. You can challenge it.

Avoid credit card fraud. Credit card fraud is a multibillion dollar problem in the United States. You can avoid being a victim by using your credit card carefully:

- Do not make mail-order purchases or give out your credit card number to individuals or companies that solicit you over the phone.
- Use credit cards for mail orders only with well-known companies and only when you initiate the purchase.
- Do not write your credit card number on your personal check.
- Take possession of all carbons used in credit card transactions. Most carbons have gone the way of the dinosaur. There are still some merchants, usually mom-and-pop-type shops, that have them. When all merchants use the electronic terminals to transmit or scan account numbers, multiple copies of transactions will disappear.

Apply for a debit card. Credit cards are convenient. If you plan to travel and need a rental car or a hotel room, the odds are that the merchant will demand a credit card. Debit cards are different from secured cards—when your "charge" slip is processed, the amount of purchase is directly deducted from your checking account. If there is not enough money in your account, the transaction will be declined.

The big plus here is that you have the convenience of a credit card and the discipline of a *finite* spending limit. It means you pay cash at the time of purchase.

Deal with credit card disputes properly. Many people mistakenly believe that using a credit card to make a purchase automatically protects them in case of a dispute. While some premium cards do offer buyer-protection plans guaranteeing products that are lost, stolen, or defective, a standard card does not absolve the shopper who uses it of the need to exercise discretion in purchasing.

You cannot "stop payment" after a purchase by notifying your credit card issuer to decline payment once you have signed the charge slip. Instead, you must wait until the disputed charge appears on your bill. Then you have sixty days to notify your card issuer—*in writing*—that you dispute the charge.

Your card company then notifies the merchant's processing bank, which then contacts the merchant. If the merchant declines the charge back and insists that the charge stays on the bill, *you must pay.* Then your only remedy is to take the merchant to court.

CREDIT CARDS ON YOUR TABOO LIST

- Cards that charge interest from the date of purchase with no grace period.
- Cards that charge interest immediately on a cash advance, plus charge a fee for each cash advance.
- Cards that charge late fees and over-the-limit fees.

A strong warning to keep in mind is that if you are in a dispute with a merchant, you must continue to make payments on your charge or credit card account. If you don't, the damage to your credit report will be worse than any gains you feel you get by harassing the merchant.

A TALE OF MS. REPORTING

One of my daughters was rejected for a car loan; the creditor's reasons were that, based on her earnings and existing amounts owed on other obligations and the fact that she hadn't reported all her outstanding debts, she couldn't possibly make payments. Sheryl was puzzled and angry. She had reported everything.

Finally the mystery was solved. Sheryl requested a copy of her report, and guess what! She found her older sister's accounts reported as hers, as well as one of mine. Of course she couldn't handle *three* people's obligations! It took a few months to unravel the mess. The end result—she got her loan.

Don't go through what Sheryl did. Preventive action is called for. By obtaining a copy of your credit report prior to applying for credit, you have the opportunity to correct errors. And they do happen often.

When you have been rejected on a credit application, you have thirty days to get a copy of your report, free of charge. Length of time will vary, depending on the reporting agencies' policies in your area.

ACTION PLAN

If you haven't received a copy of your credit report in the past year, get one at once. Make it an annual ritual—just to see what is being said and shared about you to merchants and financial institutions who query the reporting agencies. Contacts and addresses are given in the next section. Have you ever received a credit card in the mail, out of the blue, without applying for it? Or have you ever been turned down for one that you've applied for?

If you've been rejected, return a copy of your denial letter to the reporting agency with a request for a copy of your report. The address of the reporting agency will be on the denial letter. If it's within the *free period,* a full credit report will be sent to you. You now have the opportunity to make corrections or to make a statement as to what caused you to be late on a payment. It will be entered on your report. You can even direct the agency to send corrected reports to merchants who have made inquiries. Their names will appear on your report as an *inquiry.*

Get a copy of your credit report. There are three national credit bureaus: Experian, Trans Union Credit, and Equifax. If you've ever borrowed money, received a credit card, purchased a home, or applied for life insurance, the odds are that one or more of these credit bureaus has a file on you. Each has a file on nearly 200 million Americans. Their computers accept information about your payment habits from all of the major companies with which you do business. And oftentimes the information they receive is incorrect.

You are entitled to a free copy annually. If an entry that is considered "negative" is added to your report by a creditor, the reporting bureaus are

---

Although the three major credit bureaus do have overlapping files on many people, the information in each company's file may be different. To check thoroughly on your credit you should contact all three bureaus and read each report. Credit bureaus do not deny credit or issue credit ratings. They merely report your payment history to business subscribers, who then make their own credit decisions based on your credit report. It's your right to see what's in your credit report, and you should check it for errors every year. You can contact the major credit bureaus at the following addresses:

Equifax	Experian	Trans Union
P.O. Box 105873	P.O. Box 2104	1561 E. Orangethorpe Avenue
Atlanta, GA	Allen, TX	Fullerton, CA
30348	75013-2104	92831-5207
800-685-1111	800-392-1122	800-916-8800

now sending consumers a letter stating that a negative report has been received. If you have been denied credit, you will be notified and can request a free copy of your report. Do it. Additional copies will cost you anywhere from $3 to $8 after your first free one. In contacting each bureau, you must supply your name, address, and social security number, and you must sign your request. You may also be asked to supply a copy of your utility bill—something that shows your name and address on it.

What's in your credit report? Your credit report tracks payment history of any purchase you made using credit. Whether you make extended payments on credit or you always pay your bills in full every month, your payment record is reported to the credit bureau. The printed report uses a series of codes to identify your payment habits, but the credit bureau is required to give you a clear explanation of its reporting terminology. This is debated often—none of the agencies uses the same codes! If a lender has recently inquired about your credit, that inquiry will be noted on your credit report.

Your credit record does *not* include information about your salary or wages, your bank accounts, your kids, or your assets. It may not say whether you are married or not. If you apply for a large insurance policy or mortgage, some lenders or insurance underwriters request an "investigation" report, which could contain the above information as well as information gathered from business associates and neighbors about your personal living habits. In the 1990s, Equifax signed an agreement limiting investigative reporting questions.

Check for accuracy. Remember my daughter's situation. In the mid-1990s Consumer's Union asked its employees to request copies of their reports. Out of 161 credit reports, *48 percent* of them had inaccuracies, some minor, others major. This means that there is a high probability that your report has mistakes.

> Correct all errors immediately. If you are considering applying for a loan, a credit card or store account, or life insurance, or you are seeking new employment, it is critical to find out what's in your report. Mistakes can take months to correct.

Credit bureaus are under pressure to deal with errors and complaints more quickly. Eliminating them from your report can be a drawn-out nightmare. Expect to see more legislation from Congress in this area—consumers are becoming more persistent in vocalizing their annoyance with mediocre credit reporting.

If you feel a reporting error was made by a company you do business with (e.g., a department store, gasoline company, mortgage company), contact that company directly, asking that a written statement about their error be sent to the credit bureau. Many businesses send credit information to more than one credit bureau. So be sure to ask them to contact each credit bureau to which they previously made reports.

> If you feel that a credit bureau has not responded promptly (give them thirty days) and fairly, contact the Federal Trade Commission with your complaint:
>
> Federal Trade Commission (FTC)
> Attention: Credit Bureau Complaints
> Pennsylvania Avenue and 6th Street, N.W.
> Washington, D.C. 20580

You may wonder what's in these reports. Lots! Most reports will include

- what charge accounts and bank cards you have and how long you've had them;
- the date of your last payment;
- the largest amount that you've ever owed to that particular creditor or the top limit that you're allowed to charge;
- the current amount owed (usually within one month of report);
- whether your payments are current;
- the amount that's past due, if any;
- how many times you have been past due and for how many days (more than thirty, sixty, etc.);
- the type of loan or account and its terms;
- the latest you ever paid on that account and how many times you've been delinquent on it;
- any special problems with your account (for example, what goods were repossessed or when a collection agency had to be called in);
- any court actions, such as liens, judgments awarded to creditors, bankruptcies, and foreclosures;
- your legal relationship to the account (are you jointly responsible? individually responsible? a cosigner?);

- past accounts, paid in full but now closed; and
- whether you've put a statement on the record in a dispute with the lender.

Credit bureaus will identify your employer, but will not disclose how much you make. Some report if you are married. They do not give ratings, merely reporting your payment history to those who have access to it and are considering loaning you money. Potential lenders decide whether they want you or not; the credit report bureau does not decide.

Most people have good credit. Mainly what you need is a steady job with a history of paying bills on time. Your credit won't be ruined if you sometimes pay bills late. You can even hit one of life's potholes—getting threatening overdue notices—without damaging your basic creditworthiness. It's not smart to apply for new credit at a time when you're behind in payments. But once you've caught up, you'll be back in most lenders' good graces. By communicating—by phone and letter—with your creditor when you have problems, you will find they are much more willing to work with you.

Here's what lenders *don't* like to see:

- You already have a lot of credit cards, with large credit lines that have been used.
- You have been chased for payment by a collection agency.
- You were sued for money owed.
- There's a lien on your property.
- A creditor closed one of your accounts.
- You have been applying for a lot of credit lately (most lenders would then assume that you're in trouble).

Get credit in your own name. Many married women carry credit cards with their married name imprinted on the card (e.g., Mrs. Samuel Hight, instead of Sarah Hight) but find out only later that the credit card itself was issued *to* their spouses. In this case, regular monthly payments are credited to the spouse whose financial information was used to establish the credit account. Make sure the credit bureau lists you as "jointly responsible" for the credit, not as an "authorized signer" on the card.

The Equal Opportunity Act guarantees that a married woman is legally allowed to apply for credit separately in her own name. The same act says that the account must be reported without the use of titles, such as Mr., Mrs., Miss, or Ms.

Credit bureaus do not file joint credit reports; if you have credit in joint names, transactions on that account are reported separately under individual names. Joint accounts opened since 1977 are generally reported separately for each signer on the account to the credit bureau by any creditor you have transactions with.

If a credit grantor has not been reporting payment history separately, you should request a change in writing. Then check back a few months later to see if the change was made. You do not have to have a job or income to have credit in your own name. You do have to have your payment history reported separately to the credit bureau on joint accounts so that credit bureaus know you exist.

Immediately close all joint accounts (if you are legally separated or divorced). Open new ones in your own name, and then check with the credit bureaus in a few months to make sure your old account is reported closed.

> Get help before you ruin your credit. Negative information stays on your credit report for seven years, except for bankruptcy, which will hang on for a decade. You should do everything possible to avoid ruining your credit record. That means facing up to credit and debt problems as soon as they occur. Communicate immediately if you will be late in your payments.

Creditors are not bad people. Most understand the difference between credit problems caused by excessive spending and those caused by unexpected situations such as illness and job loss. You might be surprised at how many creditors are willing to work with you—if you face up to the situation early and fully.

If you feel the situation will be temporary, you can talk to your creditors about arranging an extended payment plan or an interest-only payment plan. If creditors are not responsive, or if you have too many creditors, it's time to seek help.

HOW TO TELL YOU'RE IN TROUBLE

There are multiple warning signs that you are stretched to the max and need help. Here are twenty-one reasons why you should quit buying on credit:

1. You can barely pay the minimum each month.

2. You no longer pay in cash; everything is charged.

Credit Counselors

Avoid credit repair "clinics" and "specialists" who promise to solve your problems. Don't give them a penny of your money. The only person who can repair your status is you—pay your bills and communicate with your creditors if you are having financial trouble. If you feel that you need help, there are resources. Here are four legitimate places to turn to for credit/counseling assistance today:

Consumer Credit
  Counseling Service
800-388-2227
(This 800 number will directly
refer you to the CCCS office
closest to your city.)

Family Service
  America, Inc.
11700 West Lake Park Drive
Milwaukee, WI 53224
800-221-2681

The National Foundation
  for Consumer Credit
8611 Second Avenue
Silver Spring, MD 20910
800-388-2227

Christian Financial
  Concepts
601 Broad Street S.E.
Gainesville, GA 30501
800-722-1976

Each of these agencies will put you in touch with a local office or representative that will provide consumer-credit counseling. These organizations will work with you in two ways. They'll contact or assist you in contacting your creditors to help work out a repayment plan if possible. And they'll help you understand how to deal with a spending problem if you have one, so you can avoid future credit woes.

3. The debt-consolidation loan is used up and now you're running up fresh debts.

4. You have no savings.

5. You hope the mail delivers another offer for a new credit card.

6. You're taking cash advances from one card in order to make payments on another.

7. Your basic bills aren't paid on time.

8. You dread that the next phone call is another creditor hounding you for money.

9. You get turned down for credit.

10. You buy things you don't need or want.

11. Your friends and coworkers can't figure out how you live so well.

12. Without overtime or a second job you'd lose your house or your car.

13. You're taking cash advances for daily expenses.

14. You borrow money from anyone—friends, family, coworkers.

15. You avoid opening mail that looks like bills.

16. You always choose the longest time period to repay any debt.

17. Your credit cards are never paid off.

18. You fiddle with your creditors by putting the bill for the cable-TV company in the envelope addressed to the utility company and vice versa. Or you "forget" to sign your checks.

19. You bounce checks or overdraw your account.

20. You don't sleep well, worrying about money.

21. You don't dare tell your spouse (or, sometimes, yourself) that you can't pay your bills and that there isn't enough money to go around.

Credit card issuers have developed sophisticated systems for identifying borrowers who are likely to default. They call it "behavior scoring." Here are six of the warning signals that creditors look for:

1. You pay only the bare minimum every month and never more than the minimum.

2. You make partial payments.

3. You started falling behind on your payments soon after opening the account.

4. You have taken the maximum cash advance.

5. Your account balance always grows: you can't ever seem to pay it off.

6. You have periodic bouts of late payments.

Does this sound like you? If so, your number one job is to get free of debt. It's the only way you will be financially self-reliant . . . and get rich.

If you are serious about zapping your debt and kicking the habit, there is one simple solution: don't borrow anymore! Debt doesn't have to be forever—but if you pay the minimum amount the bank requires, it may seem like it is.

Necessity is often the mother of invention. Bankcard Holders of America has a Debt Zapper program that shows consumers the quickest way to pay back what they owe and at the lowest cost. For information contact BHA at 560 Herndon Parkway, Suite 120, Herndon, VA 22070 or call 800-327-7300.

DO YOU HAVE LEVERAGE?

This leads us to another aspect of credit: establishing a solid credit rating for you and the members of your family. A good credit rating will give you leverage, or the ability for the calculated use of credit. It allows you to use other people's money to make money for yourself, just as the banks do.

Leverage is, in fact, a very apt word if you remember anything from your high school science classes. A lever allows you to exert a far greater effort than the actual force used. It can be used to lift an object you couldn't ordinarily budge. In the financial sense, it means you are able to purchase items you might not be able to afford if you used assets such as cash currently on hand.

If used wisely, leverage can work to increase the overall growth of your net worth. The flip side, of course, is that you can overdo its use. You do not want to find yourself in the position at the end of the month that the payments required to meet your obligations exceed the actual income you have available to make them.

If you find your money runs out before the end of the month, even after adjusting withholding taxes that could increase your monthly cash flow and after identifying all possible sources of income, you have a problem. If you are unable to meet your monthly cash-flow obligations, you are clearly overleveraged.

Some advisors recommend you avoid leverage at all costs. When buying a home, few people have all the cash to pay for it. A percentage of the entire price, let's say 20 percent, is put down; the remainder is borrowed. You are leveraged, pure and simple. Trouble beckons when you begin to *invest* by using leverage techniques. In real estate, if the market goes bad, you could lose everything; in the stock market, if you borrow funds to buy stocks and the market value drops, you could be wiped out of your investment.

The critical thing is to stay in balance. Think of a child's teeter-totter: When similar weights are on each side, the ride is quite smooth. When out of balance, it's extremely wobbly, and usually someone crashes!

SUMMING UP—IT'S YOUR CREDIT

Credit is not necessarily bad. It's time, though, to get—and keep—your credit house in order, to seriously attack any outstanding balances that you continue to carry month to month. If there are any errors, you must take measures to correct them immediately; they don't get corrected by themselves. Most items—positive and negative—stay on your credit report for seven years. A personal bankruptcy remains on the report for ten years. That's a heavy penance for credit misuse.

---

10 SMART MONEY MOVES TO ENHANCE YOUR CREDIT LIFE

---

1. **Get a copy of your credit report from Equifax, Trans Union, and Experian.** Identify all errors—late reportings that weren't late, accounts, liens, collections that are not yours, and so forth on your credit report. If an account has been paid off but is not reported as such, say so. Challenge anything you believe or know to be incorrect *in writing*. If you have copies of correspondence that state the debt or payment history is incorrect, enclose a copy with your challenge.

   The bureau has thirty days to contact the reporting merchant or agency to verify its accuracy. If the merchant doesn't respond, his or her report must be removed from your file. You will be sent an updated copy of your report. *Don't expect the discrepancies to be corrected with your first challenge.* It may take months to finally sort everything out. Be diligent in your quest to ensure accuracy.

2. **Limit the number of cards you have and use.** You need only a general card (such as Visa or MasterCard) and a business card (such as Diners Club or American Express).

3. **Resolve that you will use your card(s) only for items that you can pay off within thirty days.** If it's too tempting, stop using the cards. Stick them in your freezer or cut them up. Every extra dollar you get goes toward paying off the balances.

4. **Get a debit card.** It looks like and feels like a regular Visa or MasterCard, yet it isn't. Each time you use it, your checking or savings account is debited. You are now on a cash basis.

5. **Make an appointment to meet the loan officer at your bank.** Find out what programs and services they have available.

6. **Immediately call any credit card companies that you use and request a lower interest rate on outstanding balances.** For this exercise, it doesn't matter if you carry a balance or not. Your objective is to have it as low as possible if you do have balances, now or in the future.

7. **Don't pay the minimum amount due; pay more.** Paying only the minimum amounts due means you pay more over time than the item you charged cost in the first place.

8. **Find out if your credit card company participates in other incentive programs.** It's not uncommon to get airline mileage, hotel points, or other benefits when you use a Visa or MasterCard. To find out what programs your card company participates in, call the customer service number on the back of the card. Points add up to free airline tickets, hotel stays, or rental car usage.

9. **Determine if your credit card assesses an annual fee.** If you have a balance and your card assesses a fee, it's like double-dipping. Switch to a card that has no annual fee and cancel your old one.

10. **If you have credit with companies that you no longer do business with, cancel the accounts in writing and send copies of your cancellation letter to Trans Union, Equifax, and Experian.** When potential new creditors check out your credit and see that you have plenty of credit accounts available—even if there are no balances—it may count against you. Why? Because if you used all the credit that is available to you, you could max out and not be able to pay on the new account.

9

Mistakes . . . and Failure Happen

Every woman makes mistakes. Most will state that they have failed at something. My position is that true failure from financial mistakes only occurs when you fail to learn and grow from whatever the original mistake or failure was. Money mistakes will impact you emotionally, possibly physically, and definitely in your pocketbook.

When you make a money mistake, it's fairly certain that you aren't going to call your closest friends and invite them over for champagne. You feel angry, and maybe a little stupid, that you got caught in whatever created the money mess you found yourself in. Whoever told you about getting involved in the first place is probably on your "I'm ticked at" list. That person could be you.

FAILURE IS A FACT OF LIFE

To understand the feeling of failure you experience when your personal balance sheet takes a hit, it's important to understand the stages of failure. When I went through the embezzlement experience during the 1980s, losing every penny I had, I was in the dumps *big time*. I began to wonder if I would ever again do anything right. What would people think—my family, friends, colleagues, and people in the community? I thought my world was collapsing. How could I have been duped so badly?

One of the best books that has been written on the topic is Carole
Hyatt's and Linda Gottlieb's *When Smart People Fail* (Penguin). It probes
the multiple stages of failure and likens them to the stages of death and
dying. The authors cover multiple facets of failure from your being the
creator of it to its just being the roll of the dice, when there is absolutely
nothing that you can do to change it. They also write about the stages they
identified for failure, which included shock, fear, anger, blame, shame, and
despair.

According to Hyatt and Gottlieb, *failure is a judgment about an event or
events*. When a money failure arrives at your doorstep, it also impacts your
self-esteem and possibly your social status. When failure surfaces, it's common to feel isolated. You are inclined to feel that it is a unique, first-time-
in-the-universe lifetime experience for anyone. It's not.

When a money error comes your way, it is totally reasonable to feel
shock. You are stunned that you didn't see it coming, that you could have
been taken, or that you trusted someone (or something) that betrayed your
trust. You are fearful that whatever the loss, it will have a major impact on
your financial future. The bag-lady fears surface—will I be destitute when
it is all over?

When the shock begins to wear off, you are ticked. You are angry at
everyone who may be connected with the money loss. And the one you are
usually most angry at is yourself. How could you, the intelligent, caring
person you are, have been taken advantage of, lied to, etcetera, etcetera.
The deeper the anger you feel, the more likely you will look for who is
responsible for making your life hell. Then you can point your finger at
the culprit, which, in turn, leads to the blame game.

Blaming can be directed at yourself. Most likely, it will be aimed at others. When the blame game begins, you begin to sidestep some of the ingre-
dients for the failure. It may be impossible to probe and figure out exactly
what happened, to determine what part you took, if any, in the money loss.

The final steps of feeling shame (how could you have been roped in in
the first place?) to utter despair ("There's no hope, I'll never see a dime of
my money again") round out the feelings that a money failure can create.

Moving through a money failure takes time and work. You must get out
your mirror and be honest, especially when making investments. What
part did you play, if any? Ask yourself these questions:

- Did I not understand what I was getting into?
- Was the investment the wrong fit for my situation and goals?
- Did I not pay attention to changes within the money climate?

- Did I ignore advice to get out at an earlier time when I could have?
- Did I get too greedy in not selling earlier?
- Did I expect too much too soon?
- Did I sell in a panic, or too soon, because I was afraid?
- Was the person who sold it dishonest?
- Was this the wrong place to place my money in relation to my goals?

Most of these questions relate directly to you, your actions, and your attitude. The last two—was the person honest and did the investment fit with your stated objectives—are tied directly into the integrity of the individual(s) whom you sought advice from. If you answered yes to them, it makes sense to seek the advice of a lawyer who specializes in securities law; contact the Securities and Exchange Commission (SEC) or the National Association of Securities Dealers (NASD).

Now I must ask you whether, in stepping back, there were any changes economically that could have impacted your investments. Was the country in a general economic slump? Was there any major change in the tax laws that could have altered the growth capability of your investment? Did you put your money into something even though you really weren't qualified to be in it? Did you not understand what you were doing, the risks and the rewards?

The bottom line here is that only you really can know what's right for you. You must probe and explore the different money options you encounter and decide if they fit in with your profile. If there is anything in your gut that says, "I'm not sure" or "No" then don't do it.

So, where does this leave you? How about at "stop beating yourself up." Whatever happened, happened. It's time to acknowledge that it, whatever "it" is, happened and that you can't redo it. You can learn, you can remember the dynamics of what happened, and you can move on. Let me return once more to the embezzlement experience I went through. Remember that my partner had gotten in big trouble with drugs? Her trouble compounded, and it created *huge* troubles for me. I felt that I had made every mistake that anyone could possibly make. I felt like a *colossal failure* and that I would be totally *destroyed* and nobody would *ever speak to me again* because everyone *would know* how I had been taken and lost all my money!

Well, I would be lying if I said I didn't feel down and out during that time. I did feel stuck mentally. Over a period of several months (they were long, long months), I realized that my money mistakes, poor selection of a partner, and experiencing failure weren't going to destroy me. Money mistakes do throw you some stumbling blocks—guaranteed. It's highly unlikely that they will destroy you.

In identifying the top ten money fears (see Smart Money Move #1), I suggested that in rebuilding and reinventing yourself you determine

- what happened;
- what factors you could control, influence, or alter;
- what factors you could not control; and
- what you learned, the pros and cons.

When it comes to money, and the mistakes and failures that can come with it, please, please bear in mind that you are not alone. I suspect that if we lined up the women and men who have made mistakes in the money arenas, we would circle the globe multiple times. Throughout the preceding Smart Money Moves, I've identified many mistakes and snafus that are tied to fears, family legacies, a lack of planning or of investing, misusing credit, and not trusting yourself.

Outside of these specific areas, there is one zone that can dominate the sense of failure. It's the stigma of someone's knowing that you blew it or were taken in by a scam or by a con artist. This needs to be talked about. Hopefully, Smart Money Woman that you have become, you will never have to directly worry about being conned. That doesn't mean that the possibility won't show its head. And it may not be you who gets caught but someone you are close to.

There will be many times, unfortunately, when the possibility of being conned or scammed in your money life presents itself. Age is usually not a requirement. The younger you are (under thirty-five at least), the longer the period of time you have to bounce back. If you get conned or scammed when you move past the age of fifty, the damage can be unbelievably destructive.

SCAMS—THE BAD AND THE UGLY

It is estimated that Americans lose $200 billion annually to scams and frauds—telemarketing fraud alone accounts for $40 billion of this total. Occurrences intensify during the summer months. And if "the kitchen gets too hot," con artists and "scammers" move on to the next city—it could be yours.

Women, especially older women, are considered to be prime targets for scams and fraud. Once again, women have to fight back against a gender-related injustice. According to Better Business Bureaus around the country, consumer fraud is much more likely to target women. In an article in the *Atlanta Journal and Constitution*, Gene Tharpe writes, "Call them what you want—con artists, shysters, swindlers, criminals—they know how to make a great deal of money for themselves while making dummies of many people." Getting snagged by one of these swindlers is most definitely not a Smart Money Move.

An example of this hit home the other day when my friend was in down-town Denver. As she was struggling to push folded dollar bills into the slot at a parking lot, a young man approached her. He was well groomed; his clothes were those of a craftsman—he wasn't a bum. He was highly agitated and talked very quickly. His tale of woe went like this:

> *I'm a tile setter, working in Denver to do a custom job for someone who owns one of the glitzy downtown condos. My wife is ninety miles away in Pueblo and has called, saying that one of our kids is sick and has been hospitalized. My truck has broken down. It's full of my tools. My work provides the only source of income for my family. I need $45 to get a tow truck to help me. I've tried to reach my parents for the money, but they are out of town celebrating their anniversary. I'm desperate! Can you help me?*

A tear came to his eyes, and he said he had been in the cold for hours trying to get help. When my friend said she only had $20 with her and needed some of it for lunch, his reaction was amazing! He quickly pulled out a handful of ones and offered her change! Then he promised her that if she gave him her business card, she would get the cash back in less than a week. Something didn't seem right.

She declined to give him any money. She knew she had made a good decision very quickly. Why? Because a woman came up while the man was still making nasty remarks about her heartlessness. She told her that she, too, had been approached by him several weeks ago—with the exact same story. When she retold this story later that morning, two women in the office said they had given him money in the last few weeks. And the story they had heard was the same, almost word for word.

Believe it or not, this man wasn't doing anything illegal, according to the police. He and countless others know that their scams are just this side of illegal—and there are lots of potential victims out there waiting for them with open purses.

Women, especially older women, fall prey more easily because of the value system and philosophy of their formative years. They grew up believing that women should be nice to everyone (be ladylike), help those who ask for it (nurturing and nest-building instincts), and that men should handle the family money (women don't need financial skills). The value that makes them the most vulnerable, however, is that they learned to trust everyone. Think about your mother, grandmother, or favorite aunt (maybe you)—they have all been vulnerable to being duped.

The Federal Trade Commission and the National Association of Attorneys General have created an excellent pamphlet, *The Real Deal: Playing the Buying Game*. Call your State Attorney General's office for a free copy.

Get a free copy also of *Schemes, Scams and Flim Flams* that offers advice on how to avoid being taken by con artists. Call 202-835-0618 or write to this address:

Alliance Against Fraud in Telemarketing
c/o National Consumers League
P.O. Box 6580
Washington, D.C. 20035

Older women have increased vulnerability if they are widowed. They are often very lonely. A phone call or someone at the door is a welcome respite from their normal routine—day after day of minimal contact with other human beings. They also wish to prove themselves capable of handling their financial affairs, and they may be a tad stubborn—definitely women with pride.

This is unfortunate because, prior to their spouse's demise, many of them had little or no concept of the family's finances other than buying the groceries and managing the household. Making the big decisions about investing, insurance, and retirement needs was usually left to the spouse. This need to be independent in financial dealings is often compounded if widows have no children who live in the same vicinity to help them sort through their options. They are scared they will make mistakes and they often do.

Question—In what states do most scams originate? Answer—California, Nevada, and Florida! Definitely, if you don't know the person who is trying to sell you something on the phone—beware!

When my beloved Grammy was widowed, none of her grandkids or kids thought she needed any assistance with her money and affairs. She was bright, articulate, and incredibly active. I have long said that when I'm seventy-five, I want to be just like her. Grammy never just sat around, and she loved being involved with her faith and church. Shortly after George died, Grammy changed to another church. Enthused, she became the volunteer of the year. She put in more hours working in the church office than most people do at a regular for-pay job.

The congregation, pastor, and the pastor's family adored her. All of us felt that we were so lucky—blessed—that Grammy was happy, busy, and feeling that what she did was worthwhile. Grammy had so much love and caring for others, and we didn't mind sharing her with her new church family. Then questions started circulating among our family members:

Have you been with Grammy lately? ("No, she's so busy, but she's happy" was the response from each of us.)

Did you know that she had sold her car? ("Well no, but her church friends and we always pick her up, so maybe she really doesn't need a car now.")

Did you know that Grammy hardly has any furniture in her house? ("She doesn't? Where did it go?")

Did you know that Grammy is giving a lot of money to the church? ("Well, it's her money; and she should be able to do what she wants with it.")

Did you know that Grammy has given her house to the church? ("Ummm . . . this doesn't sound too good.")

By the time we all had woken up, Grammy was basically broke. The pastor was a con artist. We learned later that he and his family befriended new widows, embraced them in their nontraditional church, and then took everything they had. Grammy died several years later—her only

assets were her original family, who stepped in to take care of and support
her after all the money was gone.

An elderly woman is in particular danger when a caretaker is needed in
her home. The newspapers often carry real horror stories about house-
keepers and home health-care workers whose credentials haven't been carefully checked out. The elderly are financially ruined—some have even lost
their homes.

"EVERYTHING IS FINE"

Are elderly women the only targets? No. Men are excellent bait also. Again, it
is usually the elderly. My father is an example. Because he is eighty-eight, my
brothers and I stay in close contact with him and call him several times a
week. All of us live a great distance from him. His income consists of Social
Security ($675 a month and any money we send him); he has no investments.

When we would ask how things are going, my father almost always
answered, "Everything is fine, but I'm a few dollars short—can you send
me some money?" Just before Christmas a few years ago, he was admitted
to the hospital for triple-bypass heart surgery. We "kids" went to his apartment to tidy up and get it ready for his return from the hospital. Were we
ever surprised.

None of us had ever snooped around his place before. What surprised
us—and in a big way? There were boxes and boxes of merchandise. Where
did this junk come from and why? He was entering sweepstakes and had
bought the related "stuff"—all of it worth a fraction of what he had paid.
He had even rented a safe deposit box, a "secure" place for his winning
ticket (with his name on it) from the *Reader's Digest* Sweepstakes!

You may be thinking "So what; it's his money." Yes and no. We gave
him money each month for food, utilities, his supplemental AARP-
insurance payments, uninsured medical needs, and so forth. We had to
supplement his income because his Social Security check—100 percent of
it—always went to pay his rent. We found out that he was buying "merchandise" to qualify himself in numerous sweepstakes with the money we
had sent. As a result, he wasn't paying his insurance premiums, utilities, or
even all of his rent.

He had been hooked—the lure of easy money, money, money. When
confronted, he denied everything and said we just didn't understand at
all—he was buying Christmas presents for the family. We didn't find that
likely, because we hadn't received any gifts since being about thirteen years
old, and those gifts had been purchased by our mother. We gave him tape

and stamps to return all the merchandise, with hope that he could get at least a partial refund of the money he spent.

Two years ago we found an apartment that he qualified for at a reduced, senior rate. His pride would never allow him to move in with one of us, although the offer had been made several times. He continues to deny the facts—that he was a chump for one of the most common types of cons.

The bottom line here is that there are millions of seniors like him. In their younger years, they would be highly critical of anyone who threw money "down the drain." But now, because of age, loneliness, distorted thinking, and illusions, they become easy prey.

EASY WORK, NO EDUCATION OR EXPERIENCE NEEDED

Younger women (eighteen- to thirty-year-olds) are preyed on because they are newly independent. Many are attracted to schemes that promise quick wealth and easy ways to get what sounds like better jobs. Women without a college education or who need a second income (single moms, perhaps with hospital bills, or women laid off work) will be "easy marks" for the home-business schemes. It's not uncommon to find junk e-mail—queries to you claiming you can make big bucks just sitting at home.

The problem with such schemes is that they often require the woman to pay (cash outlays of $20 to over $1,000) for additional training to learn "new skills" or acquire "supplies." Most often the new skills are shopworn things such as buying run-down real estate, selling merchandise at government auctions, liquidation sales, multilevel sales (we suckered you in; now you find some more suckers), and door-to-door sales. All these are things they know nothing about and which will require additional cash that they don't have.

Examples of these ads can be found in mainstream publications, such as *USA Today* and the *National Enquirer,* where I found some of the more lurid ads of this type. I read some of them; if you do too, you will be appalled. With the Internet, a whole new world of solicitation and "opportunities" may find their way to your home through your computer.

WHAT DO THEY LOOK LIKE?

Here are thirteen of the more common types of scams to look out for. Some may sound altogether familiar; never fear—con artists continue to add new ones.

PRIZES AND SWEEPSTAKES—YOU HAVE WON . . .

You get something in the mail or a phone call that leads you to believe you have already won or could win an attractive prize. To collect your prize, however, you are required to do something. Usually this involves giving money or your credit card number to secure your prize. Often you are urged to buy or subscribe to something. Though it is never stated directly that this will enhance your chances of winning, you get that feeling. This is the scam that hooked my father.

Last week I received an envelope full of stamps. I'm told in big, bold letters that I can soon claim a prize of five million dollars. Who was it from? The *Reader's Digest* sent it; I have to review magazine titles among the pages and pages of stamps that were enclosed in order to find certain "prize stamps." In order to win, these must be torn out and pasted in just the right places on cards. I then mail in the cards for a "chance" to win the money.

They can't make me buy a magazine to win—that's illegal. They just hope I will think that buying a magazine will better my chances of winning. The downside is that the odds that I will win this prize are 1 in 206,000,000—which is as likely as the possibility that a train will crash through the front door of my home.

VACATIONS—ARE THEY REALLY FREE?

Doesn't Mexico or Florida sound fabulous in mid-January? You will find that airfare to the dream spot is rarely included and that a redemption fee is often required. Your "free" vacation will cost many hundreds of dollars.

This week my neighbor and I got the same Official Notification that we had won a limited offer of an "8 day/7 night Fantasy Holiday" for two to Florida, plus a cruise to the Bahamas. Boy, did this sound terrific! I'd love a vacation, and I do love cruising. But there was more to the offer. In reading the cards enclosed with the notification, we were told we would have to contact a specific Florida travel agency within seventy-two hours of receiving the notification already in our hands.

After calling to see what the real prize was, I found out that the free vacation really wasn't free. It didn't include the airline tickets for me and my husband to get from Denver to Florida (this could cost hundreds of dollars). Plus, there was a $199 handling fee *per person* that had to be paid immediately, over the phone using my credit card. *This is a bad deal.* If you get any mail like this, throw it away.

SOMETHING FOR NOTHING? RARELY!

The hustle is that merely for shipping and handling costs, you can get ter-rific merchandise. The quality is usually third rate, and it often is not at all like the description or pictures that enticed you. "Hands on" is the best way to shop unless you know the mail-order company you are dealing with.

> Don't send money—cash, check, or money order—by courier, next-day delivery, or wire to anyone you don't know who insists on immediate payment. And definitely don't give them your credit card number.

MORE FREE GIFTS—YOUR KIDS ARE TARGETS, TOO

Last year, my grandson received in his mail one dozen Wild Life Fact-File cards and an "Instant Value" sticker good for $27.95 worth of merchandise. Reading the fine print, we discovered that the merchandise was more cards, a three-ring binder, and a wildlife handbook. If Frankie sent back the sticker to claim the gifts within a few days, he would receive another gift from them, which was a baby gorilla doll. Its value was $8.95.

It took us some time to figure out what the catch was, but sure enough, there was one. We found it in the next to the last paragraph in the "Dear Friend" letter Frankie got. It said that if we accepted the free gifts, the company would send us a packet of twelve additional Wild Life cards at a "low introductory price of only $4.95 plus postage and handling charges." And a new packet would come every three weeks at the regular price of $5.95 (plus postage and handling) for a minimum of five years.

In reading further, we found that the total number of cards that they had produced could cost Frankie $1,188. It didn't take us long to figure out that if we participated in the Wild Life Fact-File cards for the next five years, we would spend a minimum of $600. That's a lot of $5.95's.

> If you get something in the mail that you did not order, you don't have to pay for it. According to the U.S. Postal Inspection Service, whatever you get is yours to keep or throw away. You don't have to spend your money to send it back.

NEED EXTRA CASH? WORK AT HOME

You don't have to look far to find one of these. Some are really dressed up as "Business Fairs," "Be Your Own Boss" and make $500 a month in your spare time. All of these will cost you money, which actually can be thousands of dollars before you decide this approach may not be your cup of tea.

SHARE WITH THE LESS FORTUNATE

Usually these solicitations are phone calls, and callers sound amazingly like representatives of a real charitable organization. The better organized "foundations" actually give money to those who need help, but most of the donations end up in their pockets as "administrative costs."

> Hang up if a telemarketer calls you before 8 A.M. or after 9 P.M.—phone solicitation is illegal at these times. Better yet, get all the information you can about the caller and report the incident. If you suspect any scam, call your State Attorney General's Office. Most such offices have a consumer fraud division.

It is rare that you will get printed materials about a charity and its administrators unless it's on the up and up. Ask for literature and check with the Better Business Bureau to see if the charity is registered. I have a friend whose rule is simply, *Never give to anyone who solicits for charity over the phone or at the door.* To this rule, I would add if it's bulk-mail, toss it.

HOME IMPROVEMENT AND REPAIR—THE FIX IS ON

Many of the repair schemes are targeted at the elderly. The spiel usually starts off like this: "We had a job in the neighborhood and some materials were left over so we can do the job for you at a fraction of the usual price."

Sounds too good to be true? Then it probably is. Roofs, furnaces, cracked driveways or sidewalks, windows, siding, and minor landscaping are the usual areas targeted for the repair services.

NEED A LOAN? BAD CREDIT? NO PROBLEM

A processing fee is always required—and the loan never gets approved. A similar scam is run on the same people who want a credit card but can't get one through normal channels. A fee is required with the application, but the card is never issued because the "card" is a secured credit card that requires a deposit of at least several hundred dollars to back up its use.

Years ago, I had a business friend who lost $10,000 in processing fees for a so-called approved $10,000,000 loan. He was angry, but he then added, "I had a heck of a ride!"

LIVING TRUST SCAMS—ALERT!

One of the newer rip-offs is directed at all ages. There are companies selling living trusts by using misleading claims and misrepresentations. In estate planning, one size does not fit all. If your estate is less than $650,000 in value, it will not owe any federal taxes, and a living trust may not be appropriate. See an expert in estate planning whose credentials are impeccable.

RECOVERY ROOM—HOSPITAL OR SCAM?

Recovery Room is jargon for a scam that is directed at a recent victim of a scam or fraud. It is definitely salt in the wounds of those who have *already* been taken for a large sum.

Here's how it works. The previous con artists sell the victim's name to another con group (or maybe the same group). The new group offers to recover the lost money for a fee, such as $200. What happens? You get taken for a ride yet again.

HOW'S YOUR LOVE LIFE? IT COULD COST YOU MORE THAN HEARTBREAK

It's divine to be in love. Ideally, being in love is a long-term state and one that is worthwhile to invest in. Unfortunately, some individuals are interested only in your money. If you (a parent or a friend) are on the rebound from a divorce or widowhood, you could be in a very vulnerable emotional state. It is very natural that you would desire companionship, but if someone is *intensely* attentive, you may need to do some checking. Especially if your new flame

- has frequent unexplained absences;
- lacks a "past history";
- doesn't allow you to meet any of his or her family, friends, or associates;
- claims to be a professional, yet doesn't go to an office regularly;

- has clothing and car that don't match his job description (the president of a company doesn't drive a ten-year-old car);
- showers heaps of attention on you;
- proposes marriage after a short time (sometimes within days);
- proposes living together, in your place, almost immediately;
- asks to borrow money;
- encourages you to go into business deals or can't-miss investments; or
- seems too good to be true.

If you or someone you know has been the target of fraud, call the National Fraud Information Center; 800-876-7060.

Your Husband Ordered It

This is one of the oldest scams, and it is directed primarily at widows. Outrageous as it may seem, the obituary pages are pure gold for many con artists. A grieving individual is identified and, when contacted, the person is extended condolences on the loss of her father, husband, son, uncle, or brother. The sales person then says that the deceased had ordered _____ (you get to fill in the blank with your imagination). It could be anything—new cookware, sets of books (Bibles are popular!), gadgets galore, remodeling, even trips. The grieving relative gets taken by going along with whatever the "deal" was. And this happens only because she wants to honor what she has been led to believe was one of her beloved's last wishes or acts. Don't.

Electronic Banking

Throughout 1999, the media trumped warnings of Y2K problems. Information, and misinformation, came from everywhere—radio, TV, newspapers, magazines, the Internet, your neighbors, family, and coworkers. Most were well-intended; some had a darker edge to them.

In early 1999, I began to get reports from listeners to my radio show, *Smart Money Moves,* that phone calls were being made to homes with alarming requests for personal data. The resident was told that the caller was a representative of the _____ (fill in the blank) Banking Association and that he or she represented their bank's task force for Y2K compliance. The caller proceeded to say that his mission was to make sure that the resident's checks and personal information matched the information that the bank had as he worked on bringing all the local banks in the community into compliance before year-end.

By the time the call was completed, information regarding social security numbers, birth dates, mother's maiden name, address, work and home addresses, and bank and savings account numbers had been revealed. The result: the scam artist had everything he or she needed to create a counter check and tap into the resident's checking or savings account.

When it comes to your money and your accounts, *never, never, never* reveal anything about yourself unless you personally know the caller. During the Y2K crossover, all financial institutions communicated with their customers directly—by mail and/or in person. The scam identified above was created via the media's hype and the customer's fear. Don't get caught.

If any of these scams or deals happens to you, remember to never give the following information to anyone whom you don't know: your Social Security number, driver's license, credit card numbers, and bar code numbers off the face of your personal checks. If you are in doubt, there are many professionals (such as lawyers and accountants) that you can contact. There are also agencies you can contact for free advice and printed materials. And they *want* to hear from you.

DON'T BELIEVE EVERYTHING YOU SEE OR HEAR

Why am I telling you all this? Because people say and do misleading things. If anyone offers you something for nothing, be cautious. It's rare that you will get something free of charge or obligation.

The above information is intended for you, and I also feel strongly that if you have a relative or friend over the age of sixty-five, you should make a point of sharing this information with the individual and encouraging the person to call you if she or he ever doubts a proposal that is offered. Be wary. If it sounds so great, why isn't everybody doing it, subscribing to it, or buying it?

GETTING HELP

Every state has a Consumer Protection Act. Use it to your benefit and for the benefit of those you care about. You can get help locally by contacting one of these offices:

- Better Business Bureau
- Attorney General's Office, Consumer Fraud Division

Both places may have toll-free hot lines. Keep in mind that when it comes to anyone marketing by telephone, you are protected by law. If you feel uncomfortable or are suspicious, contact either of these offices:

Direct Marketing Association
Consumer Services Department
1101 17th Street N.W., Suite 705
Washington, D.C. 20036-4704

Federal Communications Commission
Informal Complaints and Public Inquiries Branch
Enforcement Division
Common Carrier Bureau
FCC, Mail Stop 1600A2
Washington, D.C. 20554-0001

SUMMING UP—WELCOME TO THE CLUB

You will make mistakes. *Everybody does.* Failure will happen at some time. The odds are that seven out of ten individuals will experience a financial crisis within a ten-year period, a crisis that will most likely feel like a colossal failure peppered with guilt. Could this be your year? Any deal, or opportunity, that comes your way and sounds incredibly fabulous should make you wary. Money success comes in bits and pieces—and rarely in the first course.

The important thing is to understand that even though failure and mistakes happen, they will rarely destroy or demolish you, and you can grow from them. That means once is enough. You've learned.

---

10 SMART MONEY MOVES
TO DO BEFORE AND AFTER
MISTAKES AND FAILURE HIT

---

1. **Keep in circulation.** When bad news and times hit, it's common to retreat. Stay out there; others have been in your shoes and can help you through the experience.

2. **Don't be quiet. Report what happened.** If it's a scam, call the Attorney General in your state—that's one of the things that office is there for. You are only "stupid" if you let someone get away with any type of fraud.

3. **Buy *When Smart People Fail* by Carole Hyatt and Linda Gottlieb.**
This book will be one of the best sources to get you back on track. You can read hundreds of stories of what real people did—like you—and how they reinvented themselves when disaster and mayhem were at their doorsteps.

4. **If you have relatives over the age of sixty-five, ask if they buy anything by mail order.** Seniors kiss off money by scams that come through the mail. You will be one of the seniors someday.

5. **Don't respond to sweepstakes tickets and offerings.** I know, I know, someone has got to get Ed McMahon's and Dick Clark's money, but it probably won't be you. Once your name gets on the mailing list, you will be bombarded with just about every offering imaginable. You don't need the junk mail.

6. **Call your attorney and ask him or her if you need a living trust for your estate planning—it doesn't matter if you are twenty-eight or sixty-four.** Twenty-five percent of the population in America will be over sixty-five within the next two decades.

7. **Talk to a trusted friend and get feedback.** When you make mistakes, it's common to bite your tongue. After all, who wants to publicize that you screwed up—not you. Your friend whom you talk with should be caring, supportive, and nonjudgmental of you.

8. **Think back—identify three times when you made a *big* mistake or experienced a failure.** Obviously, you are still alive. Congratulations. Now, how did you feel when you first knew that something was wrong? What was your immediate reaction? And what did you do to (or for) yourself to move on? Past track records (that work) should be repeated.

9. **Don't give out any personal or financial information to anyone that you don't know or haven't been referred to by someone you trust—ever.** Just because.

10. **Have a massage.** Touch works. Do something incredibly nice for yourself!

Just Do It!

10

Many of us grew up with the ditty "One for the money, two for the show, three to get ready, and four to go." Unfortunately, when it comes to money, too many women stop at step three. They spend years getting ready—and more ready. They rarely go.

Being a Smart Money Woman means completing the last step. The actions you take to *just do it* will make the difference between money security and money insecurity. Doing it means that you have (or are in the process of)

- tracked where your moneys go,
- gotten control over your cash flow,
- purchased the right type and amount of insurance,
- created a will or trust (or both),
- identified investment opportunities,
- implemented a strategy of investing for the long term, and
- identified which money professionals you want or need to work with.

> Part of your planning must project out to when you want to pull back from, or out of, the work-for-pay scene.

FIGURING YOUR FUTURE INCOME

Figure that you can make an average of at least 7 percent return on your total savings and investments. Add that amount to the projection from what Social Security says you will receive (reduce the amount estimated by the government by 10 percent, just in case there is a reduction) plus any other pensions or annuities you own or will be paid. Next, look at what you spend money on. Ask yourself these questions:

- *Will the kids be gone and self-sufficient when you retire?* Let's hope so. Kids cost big bucks. Do you know how much you really spend on them?

- *Will your home be paid off?* Make this a definite goal. How would you like to just pay real estate taxes and maintenance requirements? How much does having no mortgage payment reduce your outgo? Is your home too big now so that you want something smaller, which usually costs less to purchase? If you bought a smaller home for fewer dollars, you could end up with a chunk of cash to stash.

- *Will you have less (or no) costs for further education?* This means no more college costs or training costs related to your work.

- *Will you be driving less?* You might need only one car for you and your partner; your insurance coverage might be reduced in costs; general automotive costs might decline.

- *Will you be spending less on clothing?* Most likely the answer here is yes, since you don't need a work wardrobe—have you ever kept track of your monthly expenses related to appearance?

- *Will you be spending less for convenience foods and restaurants?* Many women report that they actually enjoy cooking the old-fashioned way after they cut back their work hours spent outside of the home.

- *Will you be spending less on life insurance?* Insurance is purchased to protect dependents. If the dependents are on their own, your insurance costs should drop. Disability insurance will not apply if you aren't working for pay. It is normal for casualty insurance to also decline for home and car, once you pass sixty-five years of age.

- *Will your federal and state tax obligations decline?* If you are no longer working for a salary, your taxable income should be reduced.

The answers to these queries will most likely be yes; your goal is to have them be yes. Next you ask, In what areas will I be spending money? Trips? Learning things vocationally? Grandkids (trust me, money flows in this direction)? What, where, and when?

What do you earn today? Do you spend everything, every penny of your income? What amounts of your spending are directly related to areas that will not be in your spending plans at retirement?

When you delete the categories and amounts that will not be spent, you can realistically estimate your expense requirements for years down the road. It's this amount you need to *offset* against your future income. Your retirement income will comprise pensions, annuities, IRAs, 401(k)s, investments, savings, and Social Security. Social Security is not going to die; it may be adjusted, but not in a draconian formula as so many doomsdayers rejoice in declaring.

> Do you need a million dollars in savings and investments when you retire? Most likely, no. Don't let the media pundits and financial advisors spook you.

FIGURING YOUR FUTURE FINANCIAL NEEDS

Be wary of financial planners who tell you that you need at least a million dollars in your nest egg before you can have any peace of mind. This number, the mythical million bucks, is highly suspect.

If your kids and most of your debts are gone, your home is paid for, and insurance costs are reduced, what will be your monthly financial outgo? As much as it is today? I would say, definitely no. Unless you are planning on expensive travel to replace the moneys you no longer spend on kids, insurance, and mortgage, your monthly expenses will be reduced dramatically— most likely to the tune of a few thousand dollars each month.

Many of the financial projections by financial planning and investment institutions low-ball any reductions. The average household spends 30 percent of its money on housing and cars. When my husband and I crunched our numbers, we found that our expenses would be reduced by fully 60 percent! That's a far cry from the estimated 15 to 20 percent that was being used by some of the formula retirement projections.

The money difference between this new projected outgo and projected income is what you now focus on. Ask yourself, What do I need to make up the difference (if there is one)? How much more do I still need to make, save, and invest to supplement what it looks like I will have from my pensions, annuities, IRAs, 401(k), investments, savings, and Social Security?

It's that difference between your expected retirement income and expected expenses you are looking to create in assets. Being very conservative, you should be able to get a minimum of 7 percent on all of your investments. Let's say you find that you will experience a shortfall of $1,500 each month based on what you presently have in line for retirement income. Your question now is, "How much more do I need to salt away to create that $1,500 per month if I can average a 7 percent return on the principal?"

Let's also say that you have about twenty years until you want to retire. For an asset to generate $1,500 a month income, or 7 percent annually, it would have to be valued at approximately $257,000. What would you have to save or invest each year to get to your goal of $257,000? The answer is $12,850 ($257,000 ÷ 20 years = $12,850). To reach your goal of saving or creating $12,850 each year, you would need to average $1,071 per month ($12,850 ÷ 12 months = $1,071). Keep in mind that this number does not include any appreciation on the annual $12,850, which will get you there a lot faster.

If you think your growth and earnings would average 10 percent instead of 7 percent, you would need to set aside $8,000 per year ($667 per month); and if your average growth rate was 12.5 percent, your goal would be adding $6,340 per year ($528 per month). The greater the return, the lower the amount you have to put aside or the less the time you have to save and invest.

Summing Up—It's Up to You

Where am I going here? Simply this—get started. Today! Stay focused. Learn from whatever mistakes you make. Annually reevaluate what you are doing. Don't let anyone (including yourself) get you derailed. Finally, celebrate the new committed you.

With the redirection of your moneys, present and future, any bag-lady fears are not in the forecast for you. Are the Smart Money Moves I shared with you doable? You bet. Just do it!

10 SMART MONEY HABITS FOR
THE REST OF YOUR LIFE

1. **Know where kiss-off dollars have gone.** Ninety-nine percent of women, smart and not so smart, have dribbled away money. Your new motto is "No more loose bucks."

2. **Set up a savings and investment plan early on.** You may have started one or both already. The concept is simple, a formula that *savings + investing = money security for life.*

3. **Be consistent and committed.** It's easy for youth and naiveté to get in the way; after all, that's when tomorrow is just another day. Now you already know that tomorrows, lots of them, have come and gone. They're yesterdays. Work on today.

4. **Spread your money among several possibilities.** Savings is savings, and investing is . . . well, it does keep changing. But there are the basics. Opportunities are everywhere. Smart Money Investors learn that you don't put all your eggs in one basket. Diversifying is critical for money growth and security.

5. **Be curious, be alert, be open to new ideas, and keep learning.** Times change, things change, you change. Don't get stuck on how things used to be. A factor of what the future brings is *what you choose* to put into it.

6. **Talk about money with your friends, your spouse, your kids, and your family.** The closet of money secrets that too many families have is not going to stay in *your* home. Talking relieves and removes many of the money fears women face.

7. **Forgive yourself when you make mistakes.** Forgiveness is always easier to say than do. Some of the things that you do with your money won't work. It happens.

8. **Be smart when using credit.** You need credit and will continue to. If you don't abuse it, the credit merchants can't abuse you.

9. **Tithe to yourself faithfully.** Every time you get a paycheck, a bonus, a money gift, an investment gain, an interest or dividend payment, even "found" money—any money—salt away at least 10 percent of it right off the top!

10. **Trust yourself.** You are as intelligent, trustworthy, and competent as any financial advisor you will come across. They've just had a few more years of training and experience than you have.

Creating Peace and Prosperity for the Rest of Your Life

As I write this final chapter this fall afternoon, I'm reminded of a story I read in the local morning newspaper. A family with two children has identified itself as the winner of the weekend lottery. The take is $9 million. The kids are nine and six years old, the wife does not work outside the home, and the husband works at a convenience store. What were they going to do with their newfound riches? Head for Disneyland. Other than that, nothing.

I fear for this young, inexperienced family. The odds are that these people will be broke in a relatively short period of time. They have lived from paycheck to paycheck. They will now be prey to anyone and anything that comes along. It seems to me that there should be a string attached to these jackpot windfalls. The string should be a course on money management, so that the winners might learn Smart Money Moves, instead of being content with the Fool Money Moves they usually take. One of the moves would include investing in themselves.

INVESTING IN YOURSELF

Change is everywhere. It's in your workplace, within your circle of friends, and in your family. Best-selling book lists routinely include business and self-help offerings that charge the reader to embrace and grow through change. It's good for you.

One of the best ways to survive and thrive with change is to learn something new. According to researchers, people who continue to learn new things, skills, even trivia, are healthier. One startling fact is that when you learn new things, you are 300 percent less likely to get Alzheimer's disease. That's worth reading a book and attending a class!

When you keep on learning, you will keep on earning. It will be rare for anyone to have the same job or work at the same function for a work lifetime. Experts project that today's employee will have a minimum of five careers. This year, you may work in the health-care administration field. In five years, your background in health-care administration could lead you to a new career and position as executive director of a foundation. This year, your department may be eliminated. Next year, you may be the CEO of a start-up company whose birthing ground was your basement.

The way you get ready for the future is by starting today. The secret is to begin learning new things, new skills, and new tasks.

> When you invest in yourself, you expand your education and knowledge base. You become the creator of your future.

Today's workplace and home life almost demand that you know something about and how to use a personal computer. Access to the Internet enables you to expand your information world. The money world expands daily on the Internet with information that will enhance what you need to know and what you already know.

GETTING IN BALANCE WITH YOURSELF

One of the exercises I routinely do when I speak concerns prioritizing. People take a piece of paper, tear it into four pieces, and write down a word that would signify an item, issue, concept, or person that is important. Participants are asked to pick their top four. Then, one by one, they eliminate one until the *most important* one is left. I have to tell you, this is hard for many participants to do. As they eliminate each, it feels real. Gone, forever!

Of course, it's just an exercise. But it's an important one. To create peace and prosperity you must know what is important. Money is a factor, but not the only one. I'm an optimist and believe that if you follow all the Smart Money Moves, you will prosper.

Peace is another issue. Remember the columns of words in the first chapter on "Facing Your Money Fears"? The amount of money you have rarely is an indicator of your sense of joy and harmony in and around money. Having more will not make you more valued, blissful, or passionate. There are a lot of women who have it all . . . and are totally miserable human beings. If money is going to be a player in your life, you must be comfortable with having it and must use it wisely.

I shared with you that my family lost everything material—all our money, our investments, our home, our cars. We even sold clothes to feed the kids. Top Ramen noodles, anything to make us feel full, were our standard meals. Everybody cut back incredibly, to the bare bones, in spending. Applying for assistance was never an option for us—somehow, we would make it. Nothing was purchased unless it was absolutely essential. Few of our friends really knew how broke we were.

Once all the money, our house, our investments, our toys, and even some of our "friends" were gone, I didn't think it could get any worse. Everything we had built up over the previous ten years was gone. I was wrong. It got worse. In the middle of it all, I was diagnosed with cervical cancer and my nineteen-year-old son died in an accident. This was the time when I wanted to throw in the towel. Life was just not worth living.

But, I didn't throw it in. Nor did my family. Instead we hung in together, living and growing and giving. Our own spirituality was a factor in our growth and peace. When we opened our ears and our hearts, we discovered that there were many who were having a tough time, some tougher than ours, some not so tough. But we were all in it, struggling through each day. We had each other.

Will I ever have a million dollars again? I don't know, and it's not that important. My daughters are happy with who they are and what they are doing. My husband and I are on track to be self-sufficient before I'm sixty-five. It's in our plan for ourselves. Do any of us feel that we are rolling in money? Absolutely not. But we are prospering emotionally, spiritually, in our friendships with each other and others, and in our money moves. And that creates peace in our household.

What do we do to continue our money journey? We look for things that involve those original ten S's mentioned in the beginning of this book. Whatever we do, we want it to have a degree of *simplicity* to it—if we don't understand it, we pass. We constantly look for *solutions*—if they don't jump out, that's OK. Sometimes answers take time to be revealed.

As we get older, *safety* and *security* are bigger factors than when we were in our thirties and forties. We don't jump into things or investments that look shaky when we first peruse them—if the company's balance sheet has more liabilities than assets, even if it is a new technology field, we take a pass now because being *solvent* is important.

Stewardship is practiced in our household—toward what we have, but also toward what we give. We keep learning and practicing the art of being *smart*—we read, go to lectures and classes, and talk with our friends.

We are *satisfied* with our lives and feel that we follow common *sense* and the right *strategies* for us.

The information for you to be an incredible success is now in your hands. As an author of several self-help books, I've always felt that publishers should supply highlighters and Post-it notes with each book they sell. A book that you learn through should be marked up and written in, and it should have dog-eared pages. I'm one of those people who only loan out a book that I no longer want. *10 Smart Money Moves for Women* is written to hang out with you for *years* to come.

I trust it will be a good and true friend to you.

Smart Money Moves
Resource Center

*Get all the advice you can and be wise
the rest of your life.*

PROVERBS 19:20

Few people are blessed naturally with Smart Money Moves. They learn about them the old-fashioned way—by reaching out, reading, playing games, and making mistakes. All these methods lead to learning. And in learning about money, especially investing your money, two things occur. First, your finances increase in value, always a goal in the investment arena. When strategies work well, you learn from them. Let's look at the flip side. What happens when you lose money? Guess what. Most likely you learn again! Losing money isn't the fun way to learn, but it happens.

To help reduce your learning curve, I've assembled a library of information. Yes, I know that many of the books, magazines, and games are available in one of my favorite spots, the public library. But here's one of the money secrets I've learned over the years: develop your own library. Own it. Write in your books—highlight them and use Post-it notes. With pencil (or pen), highlighter, and a pad of Post-its, you can have millions of dollars of advice at your fingertips.

BOOKS FOR YOU

Briles, Judith, Carol Ann Wilson, and Edwin Shilling. *The Dollars and Sense of Divorce*. Chicago: Dearborn Financial Publishers, 1998.

Dominguez, Joe, and Vicki Robin. *Your Money or Your Life*. New York: Viking, 1992.

Donoghue, William. *The Complete Money Market Guide.* New York: Bantam, 1992.

Gardner, Tom, and David Gardner. *The Motley Fool Investment Guide.* New York: Simon & Schuster, 1996.

Goodman, Jordan. *Everyone's Money Book.* Chicago: Dearborn Publishing, 1997.

Hyatt, Carol, and Linda Gottlieb. *When Smart People Fail.* New York: Penguin, 1993.

Kobliner, Beth. *Get a Financial Life.* New York: Fireside, 1996.

Loeb, Marshall. *Marshall Loeb's Lifetime Financial Strategies.* New York: Little Brown, 1996.

Lynch, Peter. *One Up on Wall Street.* New York: Simon & Schuster, 1989.

————. *Beating Wall Street.* New York: Simon & Schuster, 1993.

————. *Learn to Earn.* New York: Simon & Schuster, 1996.

Mellan, Olivia. *Money Harmony.* New York: Walker Publishing, 1994.

O'Neill, Barbara. *Saving on a Shoestring.* Chicago: Dearborn Publishing, 1995.

————. *Investing on a Shoestring.* Chicago: Dearborn Publishing, 1999.

Orman, Suze. *The 9 Steps to Financial Freedom.* New York: Crown Publishers, 1997.

————. *The Courage to Be Rich.* New York: Riverhead, 1999.

Perry, Joan. *A Girl Needs Cash.* New York: Random House, 1997.

Quinn, Jane Bryant. *Making the Most of Your Money.* New York: Simon & Schuster, 1997.

Schwab, Charles. *Guide to Financial Independence.* New York: Random House, 1998.

Shaw, Kathryn. *Investment Clubs.* Chicago: Dearborn Financial Publishing, 1995.

Stanley, Thomas, and William Danko. *The Milllionaire Next Door.* New York: Pocket Books, 1996.

FOR THE KIDS

Berenstain, Stan, and Jan Berenstain. *The Berenstain Bears' Trouble with Money.* New York: Random House, 1983.

Drews, Bonnie. *Fast Cash for Kids.* Hawthorne, NJ: Career Press, 1991.

———. *Money Skills.* Hawthorne, NJ: Career Press, 1992.

Godfrey, Neale. *Money Doesn't Grow on Trees.* New York: Fireside, 1994.

———. *Why Money Was Invented.* New York: Fireside, 1995.

National Center for Financial Education. *The Reward Game.*

Parker Brothers. *Monopoly.*

Weiss, Elizabeth. *More Free Stuff for Kids.* Deephaven, MN: Meadowbrook Press, 1993.

Zillions magazine. P.O. Box 54861, Boulder, CO 80322 or call 800-234-1645.

PERIODICALS, MAGAZINES, AND INVESTMENT REFERENCES

There are hundreds of magazines, periodicals, and general references out there for you to use. Here are just a few. *Newsweek* is highly recommended because it carries Jane Bryant Quinn's column and other good money and investor articles.

SmartMoney
800-444-4204
www.smartmoney.com

Business Week
212-512-2000
www.businessweek.com

Value Line Investment Survey
212-907-1500
www.valueline.com

Newsweek
212-445-4000
www.newsweek.com

Forbes
212-620-2200
www.forbes.com

Wall Street Journal
212-416-2000
www.wsj.com

Directory of companies offering dividend reinvestment plans:

Evergreen Enterprises
P.O. Box 763
Laurel, MD 20725
301-549-3939
*Moody's Handbook of
Common Stocks*
Moody's Investor Service, Inc.
99 Church Street
New York, NY 10007
212-553-0300

Bloomberg Personal Finance
888-432-5820
www.bloomberg.com
Standard & Poor's Stock Reports
15 Broadway
New York, NY 10004
212-208-8000

DISCOUNT BROKERS

To save commission dollars on stocks, bonds, mutual funds, and other investments, many people use a discount broker. These brokers don't make recommendations or give advice. There are lots of them, and here are a few that are recommended:

Charles Schwab
800-648-5300
www.schwab.com

Fidelity Discount Brokerage
Services
800-544-8666
www.fidelity.com

Discover Brokerage Direct
800-688-6896
www.discoverbrokerage.com

E*Trade
800-786-2575
www.etrade.com

Quick & Reilly
800-926-0600
www.quick-reilly.com

Muriel Siebert & Co., Inc.
800-872-0711
www.siebertnet.com
(ranked # 1 in discount brokers by
SmartMoney and *Forbes* magazines
in 1999)

INVESTMENT CLUBS

To get all the information you will need on setting up a club, including record-keeping requirements, contact the

National Association of Investors Corporation (NAIC)
711 W. Thirteen Mile Road
Madison Heights, MI 48071
810-583-6242

MUTUAL FUND REFERENCES

One of the best ways to dig through all the numbers is by looking at mutual fund surveys and other publications specifically related to funds. Top candidates to tap into include these:

- Morningstar Mutual Funds Service, 800-876-5005, produces the most comprehensive survey of mutual fund performances. It covers more than 1,240 mutual funds, giving a full-page report and commentary on each. The Morningstar "star rating system" is based on a combination of performance and risk, and it is an excellent way to evaluate *potential* performance. The service, which comes with regular updates, costs $395 per year, or $55 for a three-month trial. But it is also available free of charge at most public libraries, and if you call its toll-free number, Morningstar will give you a list of libraries in your area that offer its service.

- Standard & Poor's/Lipper Mutual Fund Profiles, 212-208-8000, provide a quarterly survey of the 800 largest load and no-load mutual funds. Each fund is evaluated for its performance relative to its peer group during the current phase of the market cycle, as well as during prior up and down phases. The cost is $132 for one year (four issues), and this publication is also available in most libraries.

- *The Mutual Fund Encyclopedia,* by Gerald Perritt (Dearborn Financial Publishing), is published annually and includes profiles and performance ratings of nearly 1,300 load and no-load mutual funds. At a cost of $34.95, it is available in bookstores or by calling 800-326-6941. It also contains a comprehensive introduction to mutual fund investing.

A number of directories list funds by investment goal and give details on purchase requirements. A guide to funds with small or no sales commissions is available for $5 from

The No-Load Mutual Fund Association
P.O. Box 2004
New York, NY 10116
212-768-2477

Two good, overall references to funds that charge lower commissions are:

Investor's Guide to Low-Cost Mutual Funds	*The Individual's Guide to No-Load Mutual Funds*
1900 Erie Street, Suite 120	American Association of Individual
Kansas City, MO 64116	Investors
816-471-1454	312-280-0190

Two good handbooks or guides for mutual fund investors are:

Donoghue's Mutual Fund Almanac	*The Handbook for No-Load Fund Investors*
IBC Financial Data	P.O. Box 318
P.O. Box 9104	Irvington, NY 10503
Ashland, MA 01721	800-252-2042
800-343-5413	

A compilation of commission and commission-free funds is available for $1 from

The Investment Company Institute
Attention: Guide
1600 M Street, N.W.
Washington, D.C. 20036

Where there are investments, there are newsletters offering a zillion tidbits of information and strategies. They are almost too numerous to count. Most are issued monthly; some even have hot lines to update their recommendations. The prices indicated here may change. *Morningstar 5-Star Investor* is one of the most comprehensive of the lot. Its objective is to be "a teacher, a reporter, and a database." Many libraries now carry these recommended investor newsletters in their reference sections:

Morningstar 5-Star Investor
800-876-5005; $65/year

The Mutual Fund Letter
800-326-6941; $79/year

Investech Mutual Fund Advisor
406-862-7777; $165/year
(has telephone hot line)

No-Load Fund Investor
914-693-7420; $82/year

No-Load Fund-X
415-896-7979; $100/year

Mutual Fund Forecaster
800-442-9000; $100/year

Donoghue's Money Letter
800-445-5900; $109/year
(has telephone hot line)

THE INTERNET

If you have access to a computer, cyberspace holds an incredible amount of information. Once you are on the Internet, the financial world is at your fingertips. Go to "keyword" and type in *finance, personal finance,* or *money* and see what unfolds. AOL users are routinely prompted to go to *www.personalfinance.com.* There are sites for *Motley Fool,* the *New York Times,* the *Wall Street Journal,* and just about any major publication. Explore the Internet by typing in *www.,* the magazine's name, *.com,* and start surfing.

Or visit your local library. The reference section will be your guide. If you use the library, make sure the information there has been updated or revised within the last year. Most libraries impose time limitations for computer usage on the Internet. It's a good idea to ask before you log on.

Tax and Bookkeeping Software

Among software programs available for help with bookkeeping, these are popular:

Turbo Tax by Intuit (PCs)	$49.95
MacInTax by Intuit (Macs)	$49.95
Quicken by Intuit (personal bookkeeping)	$29.95
Quickbooks by Intuit (business bookkeeping)	$99.99

Smart Money Moves Dictionary

You will come across a whole slew of new words and phrases as you become a Smart Money Woman. Here's a list of some of the ones you will most likely encounter:

ADRs	Short for American depository receipts. These are "substitute certificates" for stocks owned in foreign countries.
annual report	The annual write-up of a public corporation's business for the past year; includes financial statements.
appreciation	An increase in value.
asset(s)	What you own that has value—real estate, investments, money, collectibles, and such personal items as furniture and cars.
balance sheet	A financial statement that shows a company's assets and liabilities on a given date.
bonds	A paper certificate issued by corporations and governmental agencies that borrow money from investors. In return the issuers pay interest and promise to pay all the money (and interest) back at a later date.

book value per share	The net worth of a company divided by the number of shares outstanding. The number tells what each share would be worth if the company was suddenly sold; based on the balance sheet numbers.
broker	A money professional who is also known as a stockbroker or real estate broker. A stockbroker buys and sells stocks, mutual funds, and other investments. A real estate broker buys, sells, and rents land, buildings, houses, and apartments. Both these types of brokers are paid commissions for their work.
capital	The original money you invest.
capital gain	Any profit from the sale of an asset.
capital gain tax	A tax levied on the profit of an asset.
CDs	Certificates of deposit; they are interest-bearing receipts issued by a bank that promises a higher rate of interest than it would offer for a savings account because you agree to leave the money deposited in the CD until an agreed-on later date. CDs are sometimes called TDs—time deposits.
clear title	A phrase used when you own something and don't owe anyone any money for it. It's yours.
closed-end fund	A type of mutual fund that has a limited number of units that can be traded.
collateral	What you put up as a guarantee that you will pay back money you have borrowed. If you don't, you will forfeit or default the collateral to the lender.
collectibles	Anything you buy (or were given) and save to resell at a future date.
commission	A fee paid to sales people such as stockbrokers, real estate agents, insurance agents, and financial planners when they buy and sell investments for you. Commissions are usu-

	ally based on a percentage of the total amount of what you bought or sold.
compound interest	Interest paid on both the principal (original money) and any previous interest accrued by and credited to the account. Compound interest gives a greater gain on a savings account.
debt	Moneys owed to another.
deductions	Expense items that IRS allows taxpayers to deduct from their income before they figure what taxes are to be paid. The result is that the taxable income is reduced, meaning less will be paid in taxes.
default	Not paying back a debt as promised.
discount broker	A stockbroker or a brokerage firm that charges lower commissions than regular stockbrokers charge. Discount brokers don't make recommendations on what investments you should buy and sell. The buyer gathers information and makes all the decisions.
diversification	Not putting all your money in one investment. Instead, putting a portion in one, some in another, to reduce risk.
dividend	A payment of money given to shareholders in a company. Dividends are paid only out of profits.
dollar cost averaging	Method of investing the same amounts of money over time (e.g., weekly, monthly, quarterly, or annually). You never pay the lowest price or the highest price for an investment.
DRIP	Dividend reinvestment plan, which automatically reinvests any dividends or gains of your stocks or mutual funds in additional shares of the same stock or units in the mutual fund that paid the dividend.
earnings	Any profits or income after all expenses are paid.
exempt	An exclusion from paying taxes.

FDIC   Federal Deposit Insurance Corporation, an
                            agency set up in 1933 whose purpose is to
                            cover depositors' losses that occur when
                            banks go out of business. Each account is
                            covered up to $100,000.

financial planner   A money professional who assists you in
                            reaching your financial goals; prepares and
                            writes financial plans that serve you as a
                            guide or map.

global fund   A mutual fund that invests in companies
                            that are outside the United States.

growth   What an investment does when you can
                            resell it at a price higher than you paid for it.

income   Also known as revenues; any money that you
                            receive from a person, company, bank, or
                            investment.

inflation   An increase in the cost of things. As this
                            continues, people buy less because they can't
                            afford as much.

interest   A fee, usually a percentage, paid by a bor-
                            rower for the use of someone else's money.

investment   What you purchase, with the goal to have it
                            increase in value so you can later sell it at a
                            higher price than you paid for it.

IRA   Individual Retirement Account; investment
                            accounts set up specifically to provide money
                            for retirement. Each year qualified taxpayers
                            can put up to $2,000 of their earnings into
                            this investment; any growth or interest is tax
                            deferred until money is taken out of the
                            account. Regular IRAs may be tax deductible.
                            Roth IRAs are not tax deductible, but allow
                            your investment to accumulate in value with
                            no future tax consequence.

kiddy tax   A special tax on the earnings from the invest-
                            ments owned by any child under age four-
                            teen. The earnings are taxed based on the

parents' present tax bracket. After age four-teen, a tax bracket is established for a child who has investment income.

leverage　The borrowing of money to pay for a portion of an investment. If the investment does well, you make more money on your money. If it doesn't do well, you lose a greater percentage.

liquidate　When you sell an asset and turn it into cash.

load　A type of mutual fund that charges a com-mission.

maturity date　The date when a loan of any kind is due to be paid back.

money market fund　A mutual fund that buys only other types of money, such as treasury bills, treasury notes, treasury bonds, and certificates of deposit.

mortgage loan　A type of loan taken out for buying a home, using the house as collateral.

mutual fund　An investment that pools the money of many investors to buy stocks, bonds, and other types of securities. It is managed by an invest-ment company. Some mutual funds charge commissions, and others don't. The ones that do are called *load* funds and the ones that don't are called *no-load* funds. A mutual fund is an investment that is set up to buy a wide variety of securities issued by corporations and government agencies. It is a good means for small investors to get started.

net worth　The dollar value of all your assets minus any of your debts (the result is your net worth).

no-load　A type of mutual fund that does not charge a commission.

odd lot　A number of shares that is smaller than the standard trading unit (100 shares). If someone buys ten shares, they are buying an odd lot. Investors who buy and sell odd lots usually pay a "penalty" for not trading in round lots.

open-end fund	A type of mutual fund that continues to issue new shares or units.
PE ratio	Price/earnings ratio; the price of a share of stock divided by its earnings for the past year. Many investors use a PE ratio as a measure of a stock's value within its particular industry.
portfolio	A bundle of several kinds of investments.
profit	Money left over when all expenses are paid; money generated when any investment or security rises in value and is then sold.
prospectus	A document issued by a mutual fund company that discloses what management of the company does and what the objectives of the fund are.
proxy	A written permission given by a shareholder to another person to vote at a stockholders' meeting. You must own stock in the company to have a vote.
quotation	Often called a **quote,** the price at which someone is willing to buy or sell a security.
real estate agent	or **real estate broker,** a money professional who is licensed to buy and sell different types of real estate.
recession	A temporary reduction in business activity that leads to less spending by companies and individuals.
recovery	When business activity begins to improve after a recession; when earnings increase and people spend more money.
round lot	The standard unit for trading securities. On the stock exchanges, this is 100 shares of stock.
securities	Any stocks or bonds.
shareholder	Indicates ownership in a company that sells stock.
shareholders meeting	An annual meeting that a company schedules for its shareholders and the company's

executives. At the annual meeting management presents different issues that the shareholders vote on.

shares Units or percentage of ownership in a company. Shares are entities, sometimes issued as certificates, that buyers and sellers recognize the value of.

stock certificates Paper certificates that are issued by the company when you buy stock in a company. The stock certificate will state how many shares you own.

tax brackets A percentage of any new income above a certain base income that is taxed. In 1999 the 15 percent federal tax bracket was levied until you earned over $20,350 ($20,350 × .15 = $3,052.50) was taxed at a higher tax bracket rate.

tax deferred Any earnings that are not taxed in the year when they are received. They are taxed instead when you withdraw or use the money at a later date.

tax exempt Any earnings that are not taxable.

tithe An amount equal to 10 percent of your gross income set aside for savings and investing.

trade Buy or sell units or shares of any type of investment.

unit A share in a mutual fund.

yield Also known as **return.** A dividend or interest paid by another that is shown as a percentage of the original capital investment.

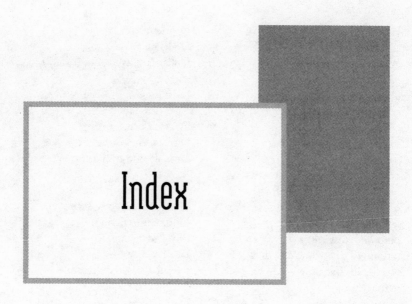

Index